This work contains minutes of an English parish council's meetings, which are in the public domain. All other parts of this work have been dedicated by the copyright holder to the public domain. You can copy, modify, distribute and perform the work, even for commercial purposes, all without asking permission.

Copyright © 2024 by Nigel Gourlay.

ISBN 978-1-913725-07-5

Published by Nigel Gourlay
Ashworth House, Long Lane
Chapel-en-le-Frith
High Peak
SK23 0TF
UNITED KINGDOM
ngourlay@gmail.com

This book is a side effect of my wish to preserve the parish council's minute books, which had suffered over the past 130 years from damp conditions within Chapel Town Hall. Those minute books are now held by Derbyshire Record Office, which I hope will ensure their continued preservation. The book you are now holding will ensure that those minutes are still available locally for perusal. – NG

PARISH OF

CHAPEL-EN-LE-FRITH.

Parish Council
MINUTE BOOK.

(Form No. 2.)

VOLUME 1
1894–1899

Minutes of Parish Meeting held December 4th. 1894.

Copy of Notice calling the first Parish Meeting

Parish of Chapelenlefrith.
Election of Parish Councillors.

Notice is hereby Given:—

1. That the first Parish Meeting for the above-named Parish will be held at the Town Hall, Chapelenlefrith on Tuesday, the Fourth day of December, One thousand eight hundred and ninety four at Seven o'clock in the evening.

2. The business to be transacted at the meeting will be as follows:—
   (I.) To Elect a Chairman for the Meeting.
   (II.) To Elect Parish Councillors.

3. The number of Parish Councillors to be elected at the Meeting is Ten.

4. Each Candidate for election as a Parish Councillor must be nominated in writing, and the Nomination Paper must be handed in at the Parish Meeting.

5. A Parochial Elector may sign Ten Nomination Papers — but no more.

6. Forms of Nomination Paper may be obtained, free of charge, from us, at Chapelenlefrith.

7. The Nomination Paper must be in the following form, or in a form to the like effect:—

(Specimen Form given on Notice.)

Dated this twenty fourth day of November, One thousand eight hundred and ninety four.

(Signed)

William Ward.
George Ibbottson.   } Overseers.
Joseph Lomas.

The Parish Meeting in accordance with the preceding notice was held in the Town Hall, Chapelenlefrith, on Tuesday, December 4th. 1894.

At seven o'clock p.m. Mr. Peter Bramwell, the Vestry Clerk, read the Notice of Meeting and asked the Electors present to appoint a Chairman.

Appointment of Chairman.
Mr. George Ibbotson proposed, Mr. William Ward seconded, and it was carried unanimously "That Mr. Joseph Heathcott be elected Chairman of the Meeting".

Mr. Heathcott having taken the chair at 7-5 p.m. the Overseers handed to him a copy of the Parochial Register, "Parish Councillors Election Order", and the copy of extracts from such order, and also the circular letter addressed to the Chairman from the Local Government Board.

The Chairman having fully explained the mode of procedure for dealing with the business of the meeting, asked for Nomination Papers to be handed to him; Fifty such were handed in, and after dealing with them as laid down in the Election Order, the Chairman read out to the meeting the names of those nominated (in alphabetical order) their abodes and descriptions, also the names and places of abode of their respective proposers and seconders.

Candidates Nominated.
The following were the Candidates nominated, viz:— Messrs. John Attenborough, James Thomas Barlow, John Barnes, Samuel James Bramwell, John Webster Cook, Tom Cooper, John James Collier, Frederick Dytor, Charles Callas Western Ferguson, William Fletcher, George Ford, James Given, Arthur Heywood, James Cooper Hyde, George Heathcott, George Ibbotson, James Ibbotson, John Ibbotson, William Anthony Bellott Jackson, Joel Joule, George William Keyworth, George Lomas (Bradshaw) Joseph Lomas (Cockyard) George Lomas (Gunstead) Joseph Lomas (Lydgate) Samuel Longson, Robert Norman Middleton, Samuel Marchington,

First Parish Meeting continued.

Edward Morton, John Edmund Potts, John Pratt, Frederick Thomas Jewson Reynolds, William Royle, Joseph Sharp, Thomas Smith, William Spencer, George Taylor, John Taylor, Samuel Whitehead, Abel Wain, William Wild, Joseph Taylor Wright, William Ward, Arthur Yates.

Invalid Nominations. The Nomination Papers of John Ibbottson and John Edmund Potts were declared by the Chairman to be invalid having been signed in each case by non-parochial electors.

The Electors were then invited to put questions to the candidates who were present, and the Candidates were given the opportunity of addressing the meeting.

The Chairman clearly explained the provision in Section 2 of the Local Government Act 1894, and as no candidate withdrew his name, put each Candidate's name to the meeting (in the order before-named)

After the whole of the names had been voted upon the Chairman declared that the following Ten Candidates, who had received the highest number of votes, were duly elected, subject to a Poll being demanded, viz:—

Results of Voting.

Samuel James Bramwell	77 votes
Arthur Heywood	76 "
William Fletcher	65 "
John Attenborough	52 "
William Ward	48 "
John Webster Cook	45 "
Joel Jowle	45 "
William Spencer	45 "
Tom Cooper	41 "
George Ibbottson	39 "

Poll demanded. A Poll was demanded by Thomas William Flanagan and by Frederick Thomas Jewson Reynolds (two Parochial Electors.

The Chairman, after Ten minutes had elapsed, and the demand for a Poll had not been withdrawn,

Vote of Thanks — declared the Meeting closed, after which a very hearty vote of thanks was unanimously voted to him for his genial and efficient services

(signed)
Jany 1st 1895 — Jos Heathcote } Chairman of the Parish Meeting.

First Meeting of Chapelenlefrith Parish Council
January 3rd. 1895.

Chapelenlefrith
Dec: 26th. 1894.

Parish of Chapelenlefrith.

Sir,

I beg to inform you that a meeting of the Parish Council for the above named Parish will be held at seven o'clock in the afternoon on Thursday the 3rd day of January 1895 at the Town Hall.

The business to be transacted is shewn on the annexed Agenda.

I am,
 Sir,
  Your obedient Servant,
  (Signed) Jos: Heathcott.
   Chairman of Parish Meeting.

—— Agenda. ——

To sign Declarations
To elect a chairman
To elect a treasurer.
To consider the raising of funds for payment of expenses incurred in relation to the Parish meeting and to the Poll.
To consider the future place of meeting.

Present at the meeting all the members of the Council, viz:- Messrs. Bramwell, Nain, Marchington, Lomas (Bradshaw) Moiten, Kenworth, Spencer, Reynolds, Heywood, and Lomas (Tunstead.) and also George Bramwell, acting for his Father (Peter Bramwell) Clerk to the Council, by right of his office as Vestry Clerk, who was indisposed.

The clerk's deputy, with the consent of those present, having read the Circular from the Local Government Board, dated 12th December 1894, the "Declarations of acceptance" were signed by the 10 Councillors present and duly attested.

Proposed by Mr. Marchington, seconded by Mr. Lomax (Bradshaw) that Mr George Lomax (Tunstead) be the Provisional Chairman.

           Carried unanimously.

The Clerk's deputy having read the notice convening the meeting (Copy thereof on opposite page) it was proposed by Mr. E. Morten, seconded by Mr. A. Wain, that Colonel Hall be the Chairman of the Council.

Amendment proposed by Mr. G. W. Keyworth, seconded by Mr. W. Spencer, that Mr. F. J. J. Reynolds be the Chairman.

Amendment proposed by Mr. F. J. J. Reynolds, seconded by Mr. S. J. Bramwell, that Mr. Joseph Heathcott be the Chairman.

The voting was as follows:—
That Mr. Reynolds be Chairman —
 For: Messrs Bramwell, Heywood, Spencer, Keyworth and Reynolds. 5.
 Against: Messrs Lomax (Tunstead) Lomax (Bradshaw) Morten, Marchington, and Wain. 5.
 The Provisional Chairman gave his casting vote against this amendment which was therefore lost.
That Mr Joseph Heathcott be the Chairman.
 For: Messrs Reynolds, Bramwell, Heywood, Spencer and Keyworth. 5.

Against. Messrs Lomas (Bradshaw) Marchington, Wain and Morten. 4.

Neutral. Mr Lomas (the Prov: Chairman)

This amendment was then put as a Resolution, and the voting was as follows.

For. Messrs Reynolds, Bramwell, Heywood, Spencer and Keyworth. 5.

Against. Messrs Lomas (Bradshaw) Marchington Morten and Wain and Lomas (Tunstead) 5.

The Provisional Chairman gave his casting vote against this resolution which was therefore lost.

For the original resolution that Colonel Hall be Chairman. Messrs. Lomas (Bradshaw) Morten, Marchington, Wain and Lomas (Tunstead) 5.

Against. Messrs. Reynolds, Heywood, Bramwell, Spencer and Keyworth. 5.

The Provisional Chairman gave his casting vote for this resolution which was therefore carried.

Proposed by Mr G W Keyworth Seconded by Mr E Morten That Mr Reynolds be the Vice Chairman of the Council

Amendment: Proposed by Mr Geo Lomas (Tunstead) Seconded by Mr Wain that Mr S J Bramwell be the Vice Chairman.

Mr S J Bramwell having declined to be nominated the Resolution that Mr Reynolds be Vice Chairman of the Council was voted upon as follows

For Messrs Heywood, Bramwell, Keyworth, Wain, Spencer, Morten, Marchington, Lomas (Bradshaw), Lomas (Tunstead)

Against. None. Carried unanimously

The Vice Chairman then took the chair and read the Circular from the Clerk to the Derbyshire County Council respecting the Regulations as to Security to be given by Treasurers to Parish Councils, to the effect that such security should be in the form of a Policy by one of six named Guarantee Societies, for an amount equal to the sum which would be raised by a rate of sixpence in the £ in the said Parish.

Proposed by Mr Geo Lomas (Bradshaw) Seconded by Mr Heywood. That Mr S J Bramwell be the Treasurer of the Council

For. Messrs Heywood, Marchington, Morten, Lomas (Bradshaw) Keyworth, Lomas (Tunstead), Spencer, Wain, Reynolds.

Against. None.   Carried unanimously.

Proposed by Mr Heywood, Seconded by Mr Lomas (Bradshaw) That the Vice Chairman and the Treasurer be appointed a Committee to make enquiries and report to the next Meeting of the Council, respecting suitable places for future Meetings of the Council, and the conditions upon which obtainable

For. Messrs Heywood, Morten, Marchington, Wain, Spencer, Lomas (Bradshaw) Lomas (Tunstead) Keyworth,

Against None.   Carried unanimously

Proposed by Mr Lomas (Tunstead) Seconded by Mr Keyworth That the Clerk to the Council be instructed to obtain all the necessary books and forms.

For. Messrs Bramwell, Heywood, Lomas (Tunstead) Wain, Lomas (Bradshaw) Spencer, Keyworth, Morten, Reynolds, Marchington.

Against — None.   Carried unanimously

Proposed by Mr Heywood, Seconded by Mr Lomas (Tunstead) That the next Meeting be held in the Town Hall on Thursday January 17th 1895 at seven o'clock P.M. and that the report of the aforesaid Committee

The first Council Meeting continued

and the adoption of Standing Orders and byelaws be then considered, and if possible, decided upon

For — Messrs Bramwell, Heywood, Lomas (Tunstead), Lomas (Bradshaw), Marchington, Morten, Spencer, Keyworth, Wain, Reynolds.

Against — None.   Carried unanimously.

The first Meeting of the Council then terminated

Signed
Edward Hall
Chairman

Meeting of the Chapel-en-le-Frith Parish Council, in the National Schools, Jan 17th 1895

Notice convening the meeting

The notice convening the meeting, signed by Mr Reynolds, as Vice-Chairman, was read, the following being the Agenda:—

To consider the appointment of Assistant Overseer and Clerk to the Parish Council.

To consider the raising of funds for the payment of expenses incurred in relation to the Parish meeting, the poll etc.

To consider the adoption of standing orders and bye-laws.

To receive report from Committee as to future place of meeting and to decide thereupon.

Attendance

Present: Col: Hall, Messrs Heywood, Keyworth, Marchington, Geo Lomas (Tunstead), Geo Lomas (Bradshaw), Morten, Spencer, Wain & Reynolds.

Appointment of Clerk to the Council, pro tem.

Mr Reynolds took the chair and suggested the desirability of appointing a clerk to the Council, pro tem.

Proposed by Mr Heywood, seconded by Mr Lomas (Tunstead) "That Mr Reynolds be requested to act as Clerk to the Council pending the appointment of Assistant Overseer".

For: Messrs Heywood, Keyworth, Marchington, Lomas (Tunstead), Lomas (Bradshaw) and Wain.
Against: None. Neutral: None.
Carried unanimously.

Chairman's declaration

Col: Hall then signed the declaration of acceptance of the office of Chairman of the Council, the signature being duly attested after which Col. Hall formally took the chair.

Confirmation of Minutes

The minutes of the previous meeting were read, confirmed and signed.

Vote of Condolence with family of the late Mr Bramwell (first Clerk to the Council)

Proposed by Mr Reynolds, seconded by Mr Keyworth:-

"That this Council records its regret at the death of its first Clerk, and respectfully offers its condolence and sympathy with the family of the late Mr Bramwell in the great bereavement that they have sustained."

For: Col Hall, Messrs Heywood, Keyworth, Lomas (Hurstead) Lomas (Bradshaw) Marchington, Morten, Spencer, Reynolds and Wain.
Against: none. Neutral: none.
Carried unanimously.

Explanation as to place of Meeting

Mr Reynolds explained that the present meeting of the Council was being held in the National Schools owing to the Town Hall having been previously engaged.

Appointment of Assistant Overseer deferred.

Proposed by Mr Heywood, seconded by Mr Morten:-

That the appointment of Assistant Overseer and Clerk to the Parish Council be deferred until the next meeting of the Council;

Salary etc

that the Salary to be paid should be fixed at Twenty-five Pounds per annum; and that the Clerk pro tem, insert advertisements in the "High Peak News" the "Buxton Chronicle" and the "High Peak Advertiser" inviting applications for the position."

For: Col: Hall, Messrs. Heywood, Keyworth, Lomas (Bradshaw) Lomas (Tunstead) Marchington, Morten, Reynolds, Spencer and Wain.
Against: none. Neutral: none
                    Carried unanimously.

Raising of Funds Deferred.
The consideration of the raising of funds to defray expenses incurred was deferred until the next meeting.

Committee appointed re Standing orders and Bye-laws
Proposed Col: Hall seconded Mr Heywood :—
"That Mr Bramwell and Mr Reynolds be appointed a Committee to consider the question of the adoption of standing orders and bye-laws and report to the next meeting."

For: Col: Hall, Messrs. Heywood, Keyworth, Lomas (Bradshaw) Lomas (Tunstead) Marchington, Morten, Spencer and Wain.
Against: none. Neutral: Mr Reynolds
                    Carried.

Place of future meetings
Proposed Mr Heywood seconded Mr Spencer :—
"That the meetings of the Council be held in the Board-room at the Workhouse, Chapel-en-le-Frith, and that the Clerk (pro tem) communicate with the District Council for permission to make the necessary arrangements."
For: Col: Hall, Messrs. Heywood, Keyworth, Lomas (Bradshaw) Lomas (Tunstead) Marchington, Morten, Spencer, Reynolds and Wain. Against: none. Neutral: none.
                    Carried unanimously

Time of future meetings	Proposed Mr Keyworth, seconded Mr Reynolds :— "That for the present the Parish Council meet fortnightly, on Thursday evenings, at seven o'clock."

For: Col: Hall. Messrs. Heywood, Keyworth, Lomas (Bradshaw), Lomas (Innstead), Marchington, Morten, Spencer, Wain and Reynolds
Against: none. Neutral: none
        carried unanimously

Notice of Motion "Division of Parish into Wards"	Mr Keyworth gave notice that at the next meeting he should move that steps be taken to secure the division of the Parish into wards."

The meeting then terminated.

Edward Hall
Chairman

Meeting of the Chapel en le Frith Parish in the National Schools, January 31st 1895

Attendance

Present: Col. Hall (presiding) Messrs. Bramwell, Keyworth, Lomas (Innstead), Lomas (Bradshaw), Marchington, Morten, Reynolds and Spencer and Heywood.

Minutes

The minutes of the preceding meeting were read.

Mr Heywood moved, Mr Marchington seconded "That the minutes, as read, be confirmed."

For: Col. Hall, Messrs. Bramwell, Heywood, Keyworth, Lomas (B), Lomas (I), Marchington, Morten, Reynolds and Spencer.
Against: none. Neutral: none
carried unanimously.

The minutes were then signed by the Chairman.

Appointment of Assistant Overseer and Clerk to the Parish Council.

On the question of the appointment of Assistant Overseer and Clerk to the Parish Council:—

Mr Bramwell proposed, Mr Lomas (I) seconded:—

"That the names and qualifications of the various candidates be considered informally and in private, before any definite proposition be laid before the Council."

For:— Col. Hall, Messrs Bramwell, Heywood, Keyworth, Lomas (B), Lomas (I), Marchington, Morten, Reynolds and Spencer.
Against: none. Neutral: none. Carried unanimously.

Informal Deliberation in Private	The members of the public who were present then withdrew, with the exception of the reporters of two local papers who were allowed to remain with the understanding that they should not report any of the informal proceedings.
	After a lengthy discussion the meeting of the Council was resumed.
	The following were the applicants for the position:—
Candidates	Jos Ford, Lower Lane Chinley.
J. W. Hobson, Chapel-en-le-Frith
Jos H. Lomas, — do —
Jno Howe, Dove Holes
R. N. Middleton, Chapel-en-le-Frith
A. Young — do —
Jno. Waterhouse — do —
A. C. Netters, Bugsworth.
Testimonials	Testimonials were received from various local gentlemen in favour of Mr Young, Mr Middleton and Mr Netters.
Election of Mr Jos Ford.	Proposed by Mr Heywood, seconded by Mr Spencer:—
"That Mr Joseph J. Ford be and now is appointed Assistant Overseer for the Parish of Chapel-en-le-Frith and Clerk to the Chapel-en-le-Frith Parish Council at a salary of Twenty-five Pounds per annum."
For:—
Messrs Bramwell, Heywood, Keyworth, Morten

Geo Lomas (T) Marchington and Spencer. Against: none. Neutral: Col. Hall, Geo Lomas (B) and Reynolds. — Carried.

Place of Meeting:- Letter from the Clerk to the Guardians refusing the use of the Board Room.

Mr Reynolds reported that he had written to Mr Boycott, Clerk to the District Council and Guardians requesting permission for the Parish Council to make the necessary arrangements for holding their meetings in the Board-room at the Workhouse, and in response had received the following reply:-

"22nd January 1895

Dear Sir,

I submitted your letter of 18th inst to the Guardians at their meeting yesterday, and am directed to inform you in reply, that they regret that they are unable to grant the use of their Board Room to the Chapel-en-le-Frith Parish Council.

I am, dear sir
yours faithfully
signed, J. B. Boycott
Clerk."

Fredk J. J. Reynolds Esq
Gisborne House
Chapel-en-le-Frith

Question to be submitted to the Local Government Board

Proposed Mr Reynolds, seconded Mr Lomas (B) "That the Clerk be instructed to write to the Local Government Board for an authoritative ruling as to whether the Parish Council has the right to the use of the Board Room" For:- Messrs Heywood, Keyworth, Bramwell, Spencer,

Lomas (I) Marchington and Reynolds.
Against: - none. Neutral: - Col: Hall & Mr Lomas (B)
carried.

Communication from the Lighting Inspectors Committee respecting transference of their powers

Mr Reynolds reported that he had received a verbal intimation from the Chapel-en-le-Frith Lighting Inspectors Committee that they intended presenting themselves at the next meeting of the Parish Council with a view to the transference of their duties and powers to the Parish Council, and later the following written communication:—

"Chapel-en-le-Frith
January 30th 1895

Dear Sir

The Lighting Inspectors have decided not to transfer their powers to the Parish Council until the end of the Inspectors year, which is on the 14th of March.

yours truly
signed, Jno Sidebottom

Mr F.J. Reynolds   Sec"

Finances and Standing Orders deferred.

The questions of Raising Funds to meet expenses incurred, and of the adoption of Standing Orders were postponed to the next meeting.

The Clerk to become a member of Parish Councils Association.

Proposed by Mr Bramwell, seconded Mr Heywood " That the Clerk to the Parish Council be entered as a member of the "Parish Councils Association for England and Wales" the Council paying the necessary subscription"

For:- Col: Hall, Messrs Bramwell, Heywood, Morten, Lomas (I), Lomas (B), Marchington, Keyworth, Spencer and Reynolds.

Against: — none. Neutral: — none.

carried unanimously.

Motion by Mr Keyworth re Division of Parish into Wards

Mr Keyworth then — in pursuance of notice given at the previous meeting — moved: —
"That the necessary steps be taken to induce the Derbyshire County Council to divide the Parish of Chapel-en-le-Frith into wards".
Mr Keyworth propounded a scheme for dividing the Parish into five wards. Mr Morten suggested three as being more feasible and introduced an alternative scheme with that as its object.
A discussion followed in which the Chairman, Messrs Heywood, Bramwell, Reynolds, Lomas (I) and others took part. Afterwards

Appointment of Committee to investigate

Mr Reynolds proposed, Mr Morten seconded "That Messrs Keyworth, Morten and Bramwell be appointed a Committee to investigate the matter and report to a subsequent meeting of the Council".

For: — Col: Hall, Messrs Heywood, Morten, Lomas (I) Lomas (B) Keyworth, Spencer, Marchington, & Reynolds.
Against: none. Neutral: Mr Bramwell
carried.

Edward Hall
Chairman

Meeting of the Chapelenlefrith
Parish Council, in the Town Hall
On Thursday February 14th 1895

Attendance — Present:— Colonel Hall (presiding), Messrs Bramwell, Heywood, Keyworth, Morten, Lomas (T) Lomas (B) and Joseph Ford, Clerk.

The Minutes of the preceding meeting were read.

Minutes — Mr Heywood proposed, Mr Morten Seconded
"That the minutes as read be confirmed"

For — Col Hall, Messrs Bramwell, Heywood, Keyworth, Morten, Lomas (T) and Lomas (B)
Against — none   Neutral — none
Carried unanimously

The minutes were then signed by the Chairman

Report of Committee as to future place of Meetings — The next on the Agenda was the Report of the Committee, as to Place of Meeting for the Council in future.
Mr Bramwell informed the Council, that Mr Reynolds was away from home and would not be able to attend the Council Meeting that evening. He also stated that Mr Reynolds (acting as Clerk pro tem) had communicated with the Local Government Board upon the subject, but as no reply had been received from that body, the Committee suggested that the matter be left over until the next meeting.
Agreed

The Report of the Committee re Standing Orders was next received

Standing Orders

Mr Bramwell stated that the Committee had gone carefully into the matter, and had selected what they thought to be the most suitable rules for the guidance of the Council

With the consent of the Chairman, Mr Bramwell read over, a list of Standing Orders, as submitted by him after which

Mr Heywood proposed Mr Morten Seconded — "That each member of the Council be supplied with a copy, in order that they might be prepared to consider the matter further at the next meeting

For — Col Hall, Messrs Heywood, Bramwell, Morten, Lomas (B) Lomas (T) and Keyworth.
Against — none   Neutral — none
Carried unanimously

Division into wards

The Report of the Committee re Division of Parish into Wards, was next in order on the agenda, but as no progress had been made by the Committee owing to the exceptionally severe weather, it was therefore decided to adjourn the matter until the next meeting of the Council

Raising Funds

The question of Raising Funds was next considered.
Mr Bramwell proposed, Mr Heywood Seconded "That a call be made on the Overseers for the sum of £25 to meet the necessary expenses.

For — Col Hall, Messrs Heywood, Bramwell, Morten, Keyworth, Lomas (T) and Lomas (B)
Against — none   Neutral — none
Carried unanimously

Motion to appoint a Committee to investigate the position & powers of the Council relating to Charities

In accordance with notice of Motion previously given, Mr Bramwell proposed Mr Keyworth Seconded "That a committee of Three be appointed to investigate the position and powers of the Council relating to Parochial Charities and Parish Property, and that such committee be empowered to obtain any advice, and assistance, which they may consider necessary."

For Col Hall, Messrs Bramwell, Keyworth, Heywood, Morten, Lomas (B) and Lomas (T).
Against — none   Neutral — none
Carried unanimously.

Appointment of Committee Parochial Charities

Proposed by Mr Lomas (T) and Seconded by Mr Morten,
"That Colonel Hall, Mr Bramwell, & Mr Heywood, constitute the aforesaid Committee."

For Messrs Lomas (T), Lomas (B), Morten, and Keyworth,
Against — none   Neutral Col Hall, Messrs Bramwell and Heywood.
Carried

Time of Next Meeting

Mr Bramwell proposed, Mr Lomas (T) Seconded —
"That the next meeting of the Council be held on Monday March 11th 1895. at 7.30. PM"

For Col Hall, Messrs Bramwell, Heywood, Morten, Lomas (T) Lomas (B) & Keyworth.
Against — none   Neutral — none
Carried unanimously

The Clerk returns Thanks

The Clerk then thanked the Council for his appointment, after which. A lengthy letter from Mr Boycott was read.

Letter from Clerk to the Guardians

Having reference to the question, as to whether the Parish Council have the right to the use of the Boardroom at the Workhouse.

Mr Boycott stated the reasons which caused him to advise the Guardians in the way he did when the application from the Parish Council was laid before the Board.

He further asked that the Parish Council would give publicity to his letter.

The Chairman said that the Council had done their duty in having the letter read.

The Meeting then terminated

Edward Hall
Chairman

Meeting of the Parish Council on Monday
March 11th 1895 at 7.30. P.M. in the
National Schools, Chapelenlefrith.

Attendance — Present — Colonel Hall (presiding) Messrs Bramwell,
Keyworth, Spencer, Lomas (B) Lomas (T)
Morten, and Marchington.

Letters were read from Messrs Heywood & Reynolds stating their inability to attend

Minutes — The Minutes were read and confirmed
then signed by the Chairman.

Report of Committee Re Place of Meeting — The next business was the Report of Committee as to Place of Meeting.
Mr Bramwell as representing the Committee said that steps were being taken to seek out a suitable place and if the Council would leave the matter over until the next meeting, the Committee might then have something definite to bring before them.
It was therefore decided to adjourn the question until the next meeting.

Report of Standing Orders Committee — The Report of Standing Orders Committee was next received.
Mr Bramwell stated that Copies of the Standing Orders (as submitted to the last meeting of the Council) had been struck off, and with one or two slight alterations (which were named) the Committee recommended their adoption.

Adoption of Standing Orders — On the motion of Mr Bramwell, seconded by Mr Morten, the Standing Orders as recommended by the Committee were adopted unanimously

Division into Wards	The Report of Committee as to Division of Parish into Wards, was next in order on the Agenda
	Mr Keyworth said that the matter was practically where it was at the last meeting of the Council
	It was therefore adjourned until the next meeting
Parochial Charities	The Report of Committee (re Parochial Charities) was the next business
	Col Hall informed the Council that the Committee had met prior to the meeting of the Council, but as nothing had been done, only the fixing of the Date and time for the next meeting, the matter would have to be adjourned.
Appointment of Surveyors	Mr Bramwell proposed Mr Marchington seconded – That a Special Meeting of the Council be held on Monday March 25 1895. To consider the appointment of Surveyors of Highways
	Carried unanimously
	The question of the necessity or otherwise, of calling an Annual Meeting of Ratepayers for the 25th March. was next considered. The Council suggested that the Clerk should write to Mr Wallis Davies (Secretary of Parish Councils Association) and ask him. whether the Council would have to call a Ratepayers Meeting or not, as there was practically no business to lay before them

The question of the Bond of the Treasurer was next considered

Mr Bramwell assured the Council. That he esteemed it an honour to be elected their Treasurer, but at the same time he could not see his way to pay the necessary premium himself. As the Office was not a remunerative one he did not think it right that anyone who was called to act in that capacity should lose by it.

Treasurers Bond

Premium to be paid out of the Rates

Mr Lomas (J) Proposed Mr Keyworth seconded That the Premium for Treasurers Bond, be paid out of the Funds of the Council
     Carried unanimously

Mr Bramwell proposed Mr Marchington seconded

Bond of the Assistant Overseer

That the Bond of the Assistant Overseer be fixed at the sum of £100
     carried unanimously

Call 25/

The Council decided That a call be made on the Overseers for the sum of £25 to be paid on the 18th March 1895

Notice of Motion

Mr Bramwell then gave notice
That at the next meeting of the Council he should move, That the Council meet on the 2nd Monday in each month for the Ordinary Meetings

Col Hall proposed Mr Keyworth seconded —

The necessary forms to be got.
That the Clerk be empowered to get the necessary forms required for the Business of the Council

Carried unanimously

The Clerk was also instructed to forward the necessary to Mr Davies Subscription for Membership in the Parish Councils Association

The meeting then terminated

Edward Hall
Chairman

Special Meeting of the Chapelenlefrith
Parish Council in the "Old Mechanic's Institute
Market Street, Chapelenlefrith, on Monday the 25th
day of March 1895. at seven o'clock p.m.

Attendance — Present — Col Hall (presiding), Messrs Bramwell, Morten, Spencer, Lomas (B), Reynolds, Keyworth, Marchington, Lomas (J) and J Ford (Clerk)

Minutes — The minutes of the last meeting were read and confirmed.
Then signed by the Chairman

The Council then proceeded with the Election of Surveyors of Highways

Election of Surveyors of Highways — Mr Morten proposed, Mr Spencer seconded. That Mr Stephen Gregory be appointed the Surveyor of Bradshaw Edge for the ensuing year

Mr Bramwell proposed, Mr Reynolds seconded That Mr Thomas Howarth, the retiring Surveyor be re-elected.

The Chairman then put the names to the vote when Mr Stephen Gregory received three votes viz — Messrs Morten, Spencer, and Lomas (B)

Mr Howarth received five votes viz — Col Hall, Messrs Bramwell, Reynolds, Keyworth & Marchington.

For Bradshaw Edge — Mr Howarth was therefore declared elected

For Bowden Edge	Mr Heyworth proposed, Mr Marchington seconded That Mr John Marchington be the Surveyor for Bowden Edge carried unanimously

For Combs Edge	Mr Lomas (B) proposed, Mr Morten seconded. That Mr Henry Morten be appointed the Surveyor for Combs Edge carried unanimously

Taking of Rooms as Office &c	In accordance with notice previously given Mr Bramwell then proposed — "That the Rooms situated in Market Street, and known as the Old Mechanic's Institute" be taken for the Place of Meeting, and Office of the Parish Council, at the weekly rental of two shillings and sixpence Mr Marchington seconded the Proposition and it was Carried unanimously

Fixing Time of Meetings	Mr Bramwell then carried out his notice of Motion given at the last meeting, viz — That the Ordinary Meetings of the Council be held on the Second Monday in each month. Mr Morten Seconded

Mr Reynolds moved an Amendment to the effect —
That the Meetings of the Council be held on the Last Monday in each month.
Mr Spencer Seconded.
The proposer & Seconder of the Resolution, consenting to support the Amendment, it was therefore
carried unanimously

Notice of Motion for appointing Committees

Mr Reynolds then gave notice —
That at the Annual Meeting of the Council He should move the appointment of the following Standing Committees :—

    (a). Charities
    (b) Lighting
    (c) Allotments
    (d) General Purposes

The Clerk having a letter from Mr Boycott in reference to the Sewerage of the Parish. The Council suggested that it be placed on record. The following is a Copy

Copy of Letter from Clerk to the Rural District Council Relating to Sewerage

To the Parish Council of Chapelenlefrith

    I hereby give you notice, that the Chapelenlefrith Rural District Council have determined to adopt Plans for the Sewerage of a certain portion of the Parish of Chapelenlefrith, within the District of the said Rural District Council, and are about to enter into a Contract or Contracts for the execution of the Works

    Dated this nineteenth day of March 1895

        John Burton Boycott
    Clerk to the Chapelenlefrith
        Rural District Council.

Mr Howarth being present then thanked the Council for his appointment as Surveyor of Bradshaw Edge. He also stated, that the Lighting Committee were prepared to hand over their Powers to the Parish Council as soon as possible after the 28th March 1895

Mr Bramwell then proposed, Mr Keyworth Seconded —

Meeting Adjourned — That this Meeting stand adjourned until Monday the first day of April 1895 at seven oclock P.M.

Carried unanimously

Edward Hall

An Adjourned Meeting of the Chapel-en-le-frith
Parish Council held April 1st 1895 in the
Council Office. Market Street.

Attendance
Present Colonel Hall (presiding) Messrs Reynolds.
Bramwell, Lomas (B), Lomas (J), Spencer and
Keyworth.

The Council proceeded to the 1st Business on the Agenda —
The voting of Salaries to Surveyors of Highways

Salaries of Surveyors
Mr Lomas (B) Proposed Mr Lomas (J) Seconded
"That the Salaries of Surveyors of Highways be
as follows — The Surveyor of Bradshaw Edge £10
           The Surveyor of Bowden Edge   £10
           The Surveyor of Combs Edge   £5

Carried unanimously

A Deputation from the Lighting Inspectors was then received.
in accordance with notice given at the previous Meeting
The Deputation consisted of the following persons —

Deputation from the Lighting Inspectors
　　Mr Howarth　　　Mr Collier
　　Mr Boycott　　　Mr Sowle
　　Mr Sidebottom. Secretary

Mr Boycott stated that the Lighting Inspectors had decided
not to transfer their Powers to the Parish Council, for the present.
And although the Inspectors had signified their intention
at a previous meeting to hand over their powers, still upon
further consideration, it was thought that the Council
would have sufficient work to do for some time, without
having to manage the Lighting Business. The Inspectors had
therefore decided to retain their powers for another
year.

Mr Reynolds and the Chairman having replied, Mr Boycott thanked the Council for the patient hearing which they had given him.

The Secretary (Mr Sidebottom) then served a Notice on the Chairman of the Council to the effect that the Lighting Inspectors were ready to produce their accounts and Vouchers for the year ending March 14th 1895.

The Deputation then withdrew

Fixing date of Annual Meeting — The Council decided to hold their Annual Meeting on Tuesday April 16 1895 at 7.30 P.M.

The Meeting then Terminated

Edward Hall

1895

Annual Meeting	The Annual Meeting of the Parish Council held in the Council Offices on Tuesday April 16th 1895 at 7.30. p.m.
Attendance	Present Colonel Hall (presiding) Messrs Reynolds, Keyworth, Bramwell, Heywood, Lomas (J) Lomas (B) Spencer, Marchington, and Wain. & the Clerk
Minutes	The Minutes of the Last Meeting were read, and confirmed. Then signed by the Chairman.
The Chairman Returns Thanks	Colonel Hall then thanked the Council for Electing him as their first Chairman. He said it had been a source of pleasure to him to act in that capacity. He had endeavoured at all times to be governed by the principle of doing the best he could for the Parish in General. And though he did not intend to seek Re-election to the Chair, as he thought that a Chairman Selected from the Town would be able to serve them better, yet he should always remember his association with the Chapel-en-le-Frith Parish Council.
Election of Chairman	The Election of Chairman was then proceeded with. Mr Lomas (B) pro. Mr Marchington sec That Colonel Hall be re-elected. He however declined to stand. whereupon Mr Bramwell proposed, Mr Lomas (J) Seconded. That Mr Joseph Heathcott be appointed Chairman of the Council for the ensuing year Carried unanimously
	Mr Reynolds proposed a Vote of thanks to the Retiring Chairman for his past Services. Mr Heywood seconded, and it was carried unanimously

Colonel Hall then vacated the Chair.

Mr Reynolds by virtue of his office as Vice Chairman, then took the Chair for the remainder of the Meeting.

The appointment of Overseers was next made

Appointment of Overseers

Mr Bramwell proposed Mr Lomas (B) seconded That Three Overseers be Elected for the Parish viz
Mr George Ibbotson.
Mr William Ward.
Mr Joseph Lomas.

Carried unanimously

The Treasurer of the Council submitted a Statement of Accounts for the year ending March 31. 1895

Resignation of the Treasurer

Mr Bramwell then tendered his resignation as Treasurer of the Council, He stated that having considered the matter fully, he had come to the conclusion, that it would be much better, if the Money was placed in the Bank and all accounts paid by Cheque

Mr Heywood proposed, Mr Spencer seconded That the Resignation of the Treasurer be accepted.

Carried unanimously

Estimate

Mr Bramwell proposed, Mr Heywood seconded That the Estimate for the half year ending Sep 29/95 be fixed at the sum of £25
For. Bramwell, Heywood, Marchington, Spencer, Keyworth, Wain.
Against: None. Neutral Lomas (J) & Lomas (B)

In accordance with notice given at the last meeting
To move the appointment of the following Standing
Committee's viz
    (a)   Charities
    (b)   Lighting
    (c)   Allotments
    (d)   General Purposes

Appointment of Standing Committee's — Charities, and General Purposes.

Mr Reynolds now proposed Mr Keyworth seconded.
That the following Committee's be appointed —
The Charities Committee, to consist of the Chairman,
Vice Chairman, Messrs Bramwell, Heywood
Keyworth, and Marchington.
The General Purposes Committee - to consist of the
Chairman, Vice Chairman, Messrs Bramwell,
Lomas (J), Heywood, Morten, & Spencer.

Mr Reynolds begged leave to withdraw from the List of
Committee's, the names of the Lighting & the Allotments.

On the Motion of Mr Heywood, seconded by Mr Bramwell
it was decided to allow Mr Reynolds to withdraw the
Lighting and the Allotments Committee's

The Proposition of Mr Reynolds was then put to the Meeting
with the following result -
For. Messrs Reynolds, Heywood, Bramwell, Spencer, Hain,
    Keyworth, Marchington, & Lomas (J).
Against. None.
Neutral   Mr Lomas (B).

Mr Bramwell proposed, Mr Heywood seconded –

Appointment of Surveyors — The appointment of Messrs Thomas Howarth, John Marchington, & Henry Morten, as Surveyors, with the respective Salaries of £10. £10. & £5.

Carried unanimously

Mr Bramwell proposed, Mr Lomas (B) seconded –

Time of Next Meeting — That the Council do not meet again until the last Monday in May at 7.30. p.m.

Carried unanimously

The Meeting then Terminated

Signed Jos Heathcott
Chairman

Meeting of the Parish Council, held in the
Council Offices on Monday May 27 1895
at 7.30. p.m.

Attendance

Present. Mr Joseph Heathcott. the newly Elected Chairman
Messrs Reynolds, Heywood, Lomas (T) Lomas (B)
Bramwell, Morten, Keyworth, Wain, & the Clerk.

The Chairman Signs the Declaration

Mr Reynolds (Vice Chairman) formally took the Chair at
the commencement of the Meeting, and asked the newly
Elected Chairman to sign the declaration of Acceptance
of Office.
Mr Heathcott did so, and afterwards presided over
the Meeting.

Minutes

The minutes of the Last Meeting were read & confirmed
Then signed by the Chairman.

The following communication had been received from
the Derbyshire County Council

                          Derby. 30th April 1895

Dear Sir
        An application has been received

Letter From County Council

by the County Council to remove the disqualification
of Mr Bramwell from being a Member of your Council
by reason of his contracting to do your printing, on the
following ground namely - that his firm is the only
firm of Printers in Chapelenlefrith.
My Committee will be glad to have the views of your
Council upon this question.
                        Yours Truly
                        N. J. Hughes Hallett

The Clerk of the Parish Council
    Chapelenlefrith

Reply to County Council	Mr Heywood proposed, Mr Lomas (J) Seconded That the Clerk be instructed to write to the Derbyshire County Council, asking them to remove the disqualification of Mr Bramwell.

For. Messrs Reynolds, Heywood, Lomas (J), Lomas (B) Morten, Keyworth.

Against. None

Neutral. Mr Bramwell.

Mr Bramwell then handed in the Accounts Kept by him whilst acting as Treasurer of the Council

Report of Charities Committee	The Report of the Charities Committee and the appointment of Trustees in respect to Certain Charities, was next in order on the Agenda.

A Report was submitted stating that the Committee had considered a number of the Charities, but they recommended that the appointment of Trustees be deferred, until all the Charities had been considered in order that the Committee might then be able to give a full and complete report

Report of General Purposes Committee	The Report of the General Purposes Committee was next received. Mr Heywood proposed, Mr Keyworth Seconded, That Resolutions No 1 & 2 of the General Purposes Committee, having reference to the Furnishing of the Council Offices, be referred back to the Committee, and that Resolutions 3 & 4, empowering the Clerk to purchase the necessary material for heating and lighting, and the necessary Stationery for the use of the Council, also the Committee's Suggestion, That the Council recommend to the Surveyor, the desirability of placing a Urinal in a suitable position, on or near to the Market Place, be adopted

Carried unanimously

Letter to the
Local Gov'nt
Board

Mr Heywood proposed, Mr Keyworth seconded.
That the Clerk be instructed to write to the Local Government Board, and enquire whether the Parish Council have power to furnish the Offices without the consent of a parish meeting

Carried unanimously

Report of
Division into
Wards
Committee

Mr Morten then submitted the Report of the Wards Comm'ttee He stated that the Committee had held Two meetings. They had gone carefully through the lists of Voters, and in the Interests of the Ratepayers, They considered it advisable to divide the Parish into Three Wards.
The Lighting area to be called the Central Ward.
Chapel Milton, Wash, Corn Heys, Malcalf, Rushop, Sparrowpit, Dove Holes, to Bank Hall, down Bank Hall road to the Midland Railway, along the Railway to the Lighting Area to be called the East Ward.
Combs, Whaley Bridge, Bugsworth, Whitehough, Courses, Higher Crossings to Marsh Hall to be called the West Ward.
Mr Morten further stated that in the Central Ward there were 360 Voters, and the Committee recommended that Four Members be Elected to represent that Ward on the Parish Council. One Member for every 90 Voters
In the East Ward there were 255 Voters and the Committee recommended Three Members for that Ward or One Member for every 85 Voters.
In the West Ward, there were 281 Voters, and the Committee recommended Three Members to that Ward. One Member to every 93 Voters.

After discussing the matter for some time

Mr Heywood proposed, Mr Lomas (J) Seconded.

Adoption of Report
That the Report of the Wards Committee be adopted, and that the Clerk be instructed to make application to the County Council for the Division of the Parish into Wards.

Carried unanimously

Mr Heywood pro Mr Lomas (J) sec.

Letter to J W Lowe Esq
That the Clerk be instructed to write to Mr J W Lowe County Councillor for this district, asking him to give the matter his support.

Carried unanimously

Mr Bramwell then gave notice.

Notice of Motion
That at the next meeting of the Council he should move the appointment of a Sanitary Committee

Mr Reynolds proposed, Mr Heywood Seconded.

The Supply of Water
That the Clerk write to the Clerk of the District Council drawing attention to the insufficient supply of water in Chapelenlefrith, and respectfully to ask that Steps be taken at the Earliest possible moment to provide a remedy.

Carried unanimously

Mr Reynolds proposed, Mr Bramwell Seconded.

The Gas Supply
That the Clerk write to the Everton Building Society, in the name of the Chapelenlefrith Parish Council, drawing attention to the deficient quantity, and the very bad quality of the Gas Supply, and to respectfully request that immediate Steps be taken to provide a remedy

Carried unanimously

Letter to the Surveyor of Highways to refuse his sanction to the Market Place being occupied by Steam Engine during the Wakes

Mr Bramwell proposed, Mr Reynolds Seconded

That the Clerk write to the Surveyor and request him to refuse his sanction to the performance in the Market place, of any Steam Engine or noisy instrument, during the Wakes, the same being an intolerable public nuisance, and the Parish Council suggest that a field would be the most appropriate place for such performances.

For. Messrs Bramwell, Reynolds, Heywood, Morten, Lomas (J), Keyworth, Wain.

Against. None.

Neutral. Lomas (B)

Mr Heywood proposed, Mr Keyworth Seconded

That the Clerk be instructed to pay the following Accounts –

Mr Joseph Heathcott		16 . 0
Mr Reynolds, postage & stationery		2 . 0
Mr C F Wardley for advertising		5 . 0
The Glossop Advertiser Company		3 . 6
	£1	6 . 6

Carried unanimously

Cheques were signed in payment of the above Acc's

The Meeting then Terminated

Jos Heathcott

Meeting of the Parish Council held in the Council Offices on Monday June 24 1895 at 7.30 p.m.

Present: Mr Joseph Heathcott presiding

Attendance Messrs G Lomas (Tunstead) Marchington, Bramwell, Heywood, Keyworth, Reynolds, Spencer, Morten & The Clerk.

Minutes The Minutes of the Last Meeting were read and Confirmed

Then signed by the Chairman.

The following Letter from the Derbyshire County Council was then read.

Derbyshire County Council
Local Government Act 1894

Reply to the application to remove the Disqualification of Mr P J Bramwell
Whereas by Section 46 (1)(e)(1) the Local Government Act 1894 it is provided that a Person shall be disqualified from being Elected or being a Member, or Chairman of a Council of a Parish if he is concerned in any bargain or contract entered into with the Council, or participates in the profit of any such bargain or contract, or of any work done under the authority of the Council

And Whereas by Section 46 (3) of the said Act it is provided that where a person who is a Parish Councillor is concerned in any such bargain or contract or participates in any such profits as would disqualify him for being a Parish Councillor the disqualification may be removed by the County Council if they are of opinion that such removal would be beneficial to the Parish,

And Whereas Mr Samuel James Bramwell, Printer and Stationer has been duly Elected a Parish Councillor for the Parish of Chapel en le frith in the County of Derby.

And Whereas the Derbyshire County Council are of opinion that it will be beneficial to the Parish of Chapel en le frith that the said Samuel James Bramwell may be allowed to bargain and contract with the Parish Council of the said Parish for work and material in the ordinary course of his business

Now it is hereby ordered that the disqualification imposed by Section 46(1)(e) of the Local Government Act 1894, shall in the case of the said Samuel James Bramwell be removed and that he shall be at liberty to contract and bargain with the Parish Council for the Parish of Chapel en le frith as a Printer and Stationer in the ordinary course of his business without incurring such disqualification as aforesaid

Dated this 8th day of June 1895

By order of the County Council

M J Hughes Hallett
Clerk of the County Council

County Council Office
St Marys Gate
Derby

The following reply had been received from the Local Government Board

Local Government Board
Whitehall S.W.
30th May 1895

Sir

I am directed by the Local Government Board to advert to your letter of the 9th of February and to state for the information of the Chapel-en-le-frith Parish Council that the Board have inquired into the circumstances of this case and have arrived at the conclusion that the Board Room of the Guardians of the Chapel-en-le-frith Union cannot be regarded as suitable for the purpose of holding the meetings of the Parish Council

I am Sir
Your Obedient Servant
F.E. Knollys
Assistant Secretary

Mr J.J. Reynolds
Gisborne House
Chapel-en-le-frith

Letter from Local Gov. Board as to the use of the Board Room by the Parish Council

---

The following replies had been received from the Surveyor of Highways for Bradshaw Edge

June 10 1895

Dear Sir

In reply to yours of the 28th May respecting the placing of a Urinal on or near the Market place I may say that I personally am very anxious that one should be placed there but I have not the power to do it but if I had the power to do it I should consider it unfair to do it out of Bradshaw Edge Rates

Letter from Surveyor of Bradshaw Edge Highways

alone. As the Law now stands the District Council will take over the Roads in 1896 and the Sanitary Authority will then have power to place one there at the expense of the whole Parish

        Yours Respectfully
          J Howarth

also the following
  Dear Sir

Letter from The Surveyor of Bradshaw Edge Highways

In reply to yours of May 28 respecting the request of the Council to refuse to let the Market Place for any Steam Engine or noisy instruments during the Wakes. I may say that I had already let it. But on receipt of your note I spoke to Mr. Hyde and others living in and about the Market Place, and they were all in favour, after my explanation to have the Steam Engine and Organ and as much of the Wakes as can be put in the Market Place, as it is an Old Custom which they do not wish to have abolished and they are all willing without exception to put up with the nuisance for the short time they stay

        Yours Respectfully
          J Howarth

The following communication was read

    Chapelenlefrith Rural District Council
      Chapelenlefrith
        Via Stockport
          29th May 1895

Dear Sir
    Chapelenlefrith Water Supply

Letter from Mr Boycott

I beg to acknowledge the receipt of your letter of the 28th inst which shall be laid before the Rural District Council at their next meeting

        Yours Faithfully
          J B Boycott

The Clerk to the Derbyshire County Council had sent the following reply to the application for the Division of the Parish into Wards.

    Office of the Derbyshire County Council
    St Marys Gate
     Derby 14th June 1895

Dear Sir

  I am duly in receipt of yours dated the 12th instant. In reply thereto I must ask you to be good enough to forward me a Plan showing the proposed Division of your Parish into Wards and a Statement giving the Acreage, and present population, and Rateable Value of each proposed Ward. I shall also want a Resolution of your Parish Council undertaking to pay the whole of the Expenses of the County Council and its members in connection with any enquiry that may be held respecting the application and order, if any, that may be made thereon. Such Costs to be paid to me immediately upon receipt of a Certificate from me naming the amount.

On receipt of the above information and undertaking I will bring the matter before my Committee, as they will not consider any application until this is supplied

    Yours Truly
    H J Hughes Hallett

Letter from County Council Re Division of Parish into Wards

Mr Morten proposed Mr Spencer seconded That the Clerk be authorised to obtain a Map of the Parish together with the necessary information required by the County Council and that he be empowered under the direction of the Wards Committee to employ the assistance requisite in the preparation of such information
    carried unanimously

The Clerk authorised to obtain the necessary information

It was proposed by Mr Lomas Seconded by
Mr Spencer.

That this Council undertake to pay the whole
of the Expences of the County Council and its Members
in connexion with any enquiry which may be held
respecting the application and order (if any)
that may be made regarding the proposed
division of the Parish into Wards

    Carried unanimously

Report of the Charities Committee

The Report of the Charities Committee was next submitted
it read as follows

The Charities Committee has had under its consideration the
whole of the Charities relating to Chapel en le frith Parish and
submit the following Recommendations to the Council
viz — With respect to the three Educational Charities
Dixons, Kirks, and Marchingtons, which bring in at
present a total income of £27.9.8 pr annum and
of which the Vicar and Churchwardens are Trustees,
The Committee recommend that Mr Ebenezer Hyde
Market Place Chapel en le frith, and Mr James Thomason
of Town End, Chapel en le frith be appointed Trustees
in place of Churchwardens,

With respect to the following 11 Charities viz —
Walkers. Bowdens. Bradshaws. Dains. Vernons. Mossleys.
Gees. Gaskells. J Barbers. Radcliffe's. Needhams.
which bring in a total income of £27.19.0 pr annum
and of which the Churchwardens and Overseers, have hitherto
acted as Trustees, The Committee recommend that
Mr Joseph Heathcott of Chapel en le frith, M F.J.J. Reynolds of
Chapel en le frith, Mr George Lomas of Tunstead Farm, and
Mr G. W. Keyworth of Dove Holes be appointed Trustees
in place of Churchwardens and Overseers.

With respect to the following 2 Charities viz
Hibberts and Kirks. Total income £5-15-0 which
is applied to an apprentice Fund, the Churchwardens
and Overseers acting as Trustees. The Committee
recommend the same Trustees as for the preceding
11 Charities.

With respect to Frith's Charity, representing a total
Sum of £125 of which no trace can now be found
but which appears (according to a Report of the
Charity Commissioners) to have been in existence
in 1835. The Committee recommend that the
Charity Commissioners be asked what steps it
is possible to take towards the recovery of the
Charity.

With respect to the remaining Charities viz —
Moseleys. W Barbers. Woods. Marshalls. Scholes.
Gisbornes. Parish Land. Bowden Head School.
(Some of which are Ecclesiastical) sufficient
information, has not yet been obtained to enable
the Committee to make any recommendation.

Appointment of Trustees

Mr Bramwell proposed Mr Mosten Seconded
That Mr Ebenezer Hyde & Mr James Thomason be
appointed Trustees for the following Educational Charities
viz, Dixons. Marchington. Kirks, in place of
the Churchwardens

Carried unanimously

Appointment of Trustees

Mr Heywood proposed Mr Keyworth Seconded
That Mr Joseph Heathcote, Mr F. J. J. Reynolds. Mr Geo Lomas.
and Mr G W Keyworth, be appointed Trustees to the
following Eleven Charities viz Walkers. Bowdens. Bradshaws. Davis.
Vernons. Moseleys. Gees. Gaskells. J Barbers. Radcliffes. Needhams.

Carried unanimously

Also proposed by Mr Bramwell Seconded by Mr Morten That the Same Persons be appointed Trustees for Hibberts and Kirks Charity as for the preceding 11 Charities

Carried unanimously

Adoption of the Report

Mr Heathcott proposed Mr Heywood Seconded That the Charity Committee's Report be adopted

Carried unanimously

The following application was read

Chapel-en-le-frith
June 7 1895

Dear Sir

We the undersigned Parishioners of Chapel-en-le-frith have a desire to procure Small plots of Land for Gardening

Application for Allotments

purposes under the Allotments Act. We therefore most respectfully wish You to bring the matter before your Council at your Earliest Convenience. For the purpose of discussing the advisability of putting the said act into Operation in this Town. If suitable, conveniently Situated Land can be procured by Your Council for the above named purpose so that we could occupy about the end of this Year or very early in 1896. By doing so we feel sure Your Council would be providing for a long felt want in Chapel-en-le-frith and the efforts of the Council in this matter would be highly appreciated by the Whole of the inhabitants. We therefore trust that this requisition will meet with the unanimous approval and Support of the Council. By giving your kind attention and support to this matter we shall esteem it a great favour

Yours most Respectfully

J. J. Bamford   Gill Townson
F. A. Wigley   Mark Hart
S Shingler   E Hibbert
Alfred King   H. Saunders
W H White   A. Simmonds
M Frost   John Sowle
W Crossland   George Street
        George Sturgeon

Appointment of An Allotments Committee

Mr Reynolds proposed   Mr Heywood seconded
That Messrs Heathcott, Heywood, Morten, Spencer, Wain, Reynolds & Bramwell, be appointed a Committee to ascertain the Views of the Requisitionists as to the amount of Rent they would be willing to pay for allotments & the Situation of available Land. Also to obtain such general information as will assist the Council in coming to a decision upon the Matter.

Carried unanimously

Mr Heathcott proposed   Mr Morten seconded
That the Clerk be instructed to obtain a Copy of the Allotments Acts of 1887 and 1890 and of the Charitable Trusts Acts of 1855 and 1860

Carried unanimously

No Reply from the Gas Company

The fact of the Everton Building Society not having replied to the Council's Letter of May 28 gave rise to some comments. The Council were unanimous in their opinion that they were not being treated by the Gas Company in a Courteous Manner

Appointment of a Sanitary Committee

In accordance with notice given at the last meeting Mr Bramwell then proposed and Mr Morten Sec That a Sanitary Committee be appointed consisting of the Chairman, Vice Chairman, Messrs Heywood, Spencer, Bramwell & Lomas (Tunstead).

Such Committee to take any action they may consider necessary to protect the health of the inhabitants of this Parish

Carried unanimously

A letter having been read from Sparrowpit calling attention to the unsatisfactory condition of the supply of pure water —

On the motion of Mr Bramwell seconded by Mr Morten it was unanimously resolved —

That the letter be acknowledged, and attention promised

The meeting then terminated

Jos Heathcott
Chairman

Meeting of the Parish Council in the Council Office on Monday Aug 26 1894 at 7.30 p.m.

Attendance — Present — Mr Joseph Heathcott (presiding) Messrs Reynolds, Bramwell, Lomas (J) Lomas (B) Martin, Keyworth, & The Clerk.

Minutes — The Minutes of the preceding were read, and Confirmed.
Then signed by the Chairman

Letter from Mr Hyde & Mr Thomason — Letters were read from Mr Ebenezer Hyde and Mr James Thomason, expressing their thanks for the honour conferred upon them at the last meeting of the Council by Electing them Trustees of the Educational Charities, vz Dixons, Kirks, and Mackingtons.

Reply from Local Government Board — A Letter from the Local Government Board was read, referring to the question of the Parish Council as to whether the Council could furnish Offices without the Consent of a Parish Meeting.
The Local Government Board's Reply was favourable to the Council, whereupon

Resolution Empowering the General Purposes Committee to Rent Two Rooms — Mr Keyworth proposed Mr Martin seconded that the General Purposes Committee be empowered to rent from the Savings Bank Trustees for the Parish Council, on the most reasonable Terms possible, the Two Rooms available in the Town Hall, and to purchase the requisite Furnishings
carried unanimously

The Reports of Committees were next received.

Report of Committee

Mr Moden reported that the Wards Committee had met and had instructed the Clerk to procure a Map of the Parish and mark thereon the Divisions of the proposed Wards, also to obtain the Rateable Value, the Acreage, and Population of each proposed Ward and submit the same to the County Council.

Report of Comttee (Allotment)

Mr Heathcott as chairman of the Allotments Committee stated that an Interview was arranged with a Deputation from the Requisitionists, which took place in due course. It was then learned that the Applicants desired to obtain land situated above or below the Midland Station, to the extent of about half a rood each, for which they would be willing to pay at the rate of 7/6 to 10/- per half rood.

Subsequently the views of the several owners concerned were ascertained, and it appears that there is not any likelihood of the desired land being obtained at such a price as would meet the wishes of the applicants.

The Committee were making further inquiries with the object of ascertaining what other land might be available for the required purpose, and when that information was gathered it was proposed to again meet the requisitionists, and also to present a further report to a later meeting of the Council.

The Assistant Overseer submitted the names of Mr John Jackson and Mr Edward Ford as his bondsmen subject to the approval of the Parish Council.

Acceptance of the Assistant Overseers Sureties

Mr Bramwell proposed Mr Lomas (J) seconded That the Parish Council accepts the persons of Edward Ford and John Jackson (as sureties for the good conduct of the Assistant Overseer) Jointly in the sum of £100

carried unanimously

Notice of Motion

Mr Bramwell then gave notice. That at the next Meeting he should move the appointment of a Finance Committee composed of the Chairman & Vice Chairman

Accounts

On the Motion of Mr Reynolds seconded by Mr Morten it was Resolved that the Account of Mr S J Bramwell Printer & Stationer for the sum of £4-0-11 be passed

Special Meeting of the Parish Council
in the Council Office on Monday Sep 9 1895

Present Mr Joseph Heathcott (presiding)
Messrs Reynolds, Bramwell, Morten, Keyworth,
Lomas (J), Lomas (B) & The Clerk

The Chairman explained the object of the
Meeting by reading the following requisition
which he had received

  Smithfield House
    Chapelenlefrith
      Sep 4 1895
We understand that an Encroachment is
being made upon public Land, in the rebuilding
of Two Cottages on Church Brow by Mrs Walton
and we beg to call the attention of the
Parish Council to the same.
    Yours Very Truly
     Jas C Hyde
     Ebenezer Hyde
     Thos Carrington
     George Ford
     S J Bramwell

To Joseph Heathcott Esq
  The Chairman of the
    Parish Council. Chapelenlefrith.

After discussing the matter for some time
The Council went to view the site of the
alleged encroachment. On their return

Mr Reynolds proposed Mr Keyworth seconded

That the following reply be sent to the Requisitionists —

Reply sent to the Requisitionists

The Parish Council having fully investigated the question raised in your communication of the 4th inst, has come to the conclusion that in its opinion the plans for the proposed Erection show an undoubted encroachment upon the public right of way. Further that in consideration of the fact that the existing way will be in one place widened by the proposed new building, and further that Mrs Walton is prepared to take down the Brick Building now existing and to restore the site thereof to the road, and further that from a Sanitary point of view the new erection would be an improvement; the Council considers that in this case it is not desirable for it at present to take any action in the matter

Carried unanimously

It was also proposed by Mr Lomas (J) and Seconded by Mr Keyworth

Copy to be sent to the District Council

That the Clerk write to the District Council and inform them of the Parish Council having received a complaint of an alleged encroachment being made, and also to forward to the District Council a Copy of the Parish Councils Reply to the requisitionists —

Carried unanimously

Jos Heathcott

Meeting of the Parish Council held in the Council Room Town Hall on Monday October 28 1895

Present: Mr Joseph Heathcott (presiding)

Attendance — Messrs Heywood, Reynolds, Bramwell, Lomas (J), Keyworth, Spencer & The Clerk.

Mr Reynolds made allusion to the fact of the Chairman having been made a Justice of the Peace, a matter to which Mr Heywood & Bramwell also referred in complimentary terms.

The Chairman responded and thanked the Members of the Council for their very kind expressions.

Minutes — The Minutes of the Two preceding Meetings of the Council were read and confirmed. Then signed by the Chairman.

Letter to the Charity Commissioners — Mr Heywood proposed, Mr Spencer seconded That the Charity Commissioners be written to informing them that the time is drawing near when the various Charities are dispensed and asking them to confirm the appointment of Trustees, the names of whom had been submitted to them.

Carried unanimously

Report of G.P. Com tee — Mr Bramwell proposed Mr Keyworth sec That the Report of the General Purposes Com tee having reference to the renting of the Two Rooms at the Town Hall for £4 per annum be adopted

Carried unanimously

Mr Heywood, pro Mr Lomas. Sec

Report of Allot's Com tee
That the Report of the Allotments Com tee be adopted
                    Carried unanimously

Mr Reynolds, pro Mr Keyworth, Sec

Report of Wards Committee
That the Report of the Wards Com tee be adopted
That Com tee having supplied the County Council
with the necessary particulars which were as
follows. —

    Acreage   Central Ward 269 Acres
                  East Ward   4759   "
                  West   "   4723   "

    Estimated population
                  Central 1857
                  East   1330
                  West   1460

    Rateable Value
            Central Ward £5039 - 10
            East   "   £11917 . 13 - 6
            West   "   £8734

                  Carried unanimously

Appointment of Finance Com tee
In accordance with notice of Motion given at the last
meeting Mr Bramwell proposed
    That a Finance Com tee be appointed consisting
of the Chairman & Vice Chairman
Mr Heywood Sec and it was carried unanimously

Mr Heywood pro   Mr Spencer sec

Letter to the Surveyor of Highways
That a letter be written to the Surveyor, calling his attention to the unsatisfactory condition in which the contractors are leaving the parish Highways

Carried unanimously

Mr Reynolds pro   Mr Bramwell sec.

Defective Supply and quality of Gas
That the Parish Council draws the attention of the Lighting Inspectors to the continued defective supply and quality of the Gas in the Town, and to the great annoyance and inconvenience resulting therefrom and further respectfully suggests that the Inspectors should make representations to the owners of the Gas Works and inform them that unless the matter receives immediate attention stringent measures will be taken forthwith.

Carried unanimously.

Mr Bramwell pro   Mr Spencer sec

Precept %32
That a precept be issued upon the Overseers for the sum of £25.

Carried unanimously.

Mr Heywood pro   Mr Bramwell sec

Accounts %32
That the account of Mrs Willcock to the amount of £3-17-6 be paid

Carried unanimously

Jos Walkett

Meeting of the Parish Council in the Council Room Town Hall on Monday A. Dec't 2nd /95

Present — Mr Joseph Heathcott (presiding)

Attendance — Messrs Heywood, Bramwell, Morten, Keyworth, Lomas (J) Lomas (B) & the Clerk

Minutes — The minutes of the Last Meeting were read & Confirmed Then signed by the Chairman.

Proposed by Mr Bramwell. Seconded by Mr Heywood

Adoption of the Small Tenements Rating Act for the Sanitary Rate — That in the Case of the Special Rate for Sanitary purposes the Owners be rated instead of the Occupiers, for Small Tenements, Rateable Value not exceeding £8 under the Small Tenements Rating Act.

For Messrs Bramwell, Heywood, Morten, Keyworth.
Against. None
Neutral. Lomas (J). Lomas (B).

Correspondence — Letters were read from the Everton & West Derby Building Society and also from Mr Howarth Surveyor of Highways in Reply to the Resolutions passed at the last meeting of the Council, a copy of such resolutions having been sent to the respective Parties.

Mr Heathcott proposed Mr Lomas (J) Sec
That the Report of the Allotments Com'tee be adopted.
Carried unanimously.

Appointment of Members to attend the Inquiry — Proposed by Mr Lomas (J) Seconded by Mr Lomas (B) That the Wards Committee, along with Mr Heathcott & Mr Heywood be appointed to attend the Inquiry on Dec 5/95 Relating to the Division of the Parish into Wards.
Carried unanimously

Mr Keyworth proposed. Mr Heywood Sec.

Refuse Tip for Dove holes — That the District Council be asked to provide a refuse Tip for Dove holes district.
Carried unanimously.

Accounts Mr Heywood proposed Mr Lomas (J) Sec
Ch.2   That the accounts of Mr Heafield & the Clerk amounting
       to £1.5.4 be paid
                carried unanimously.

                        Jos Heathcott
                              Chairman

Meeting of the Parish Council in the Council Room Town Hall on Monday December 30th 1895.

Present: Mr Joseph Heathcott (presiding)

Attendance — Messrs Heywood, Morten, Keyworth, Lomas (B) & The Clerk

Minutes — The minutes of the last Meeting were read and confirmed. Then signed by the Chairman.

Letter from Mr Boycott — A letter from Mr Boycott was read in reply to the communication sent from the Parish Council in reference to the providing of a Refuse Tip for Dove Holes district.

Letter from the Charity Commissioners — Also a lengthy letter from the Charity Commissioners having reference to the Parish Charities.

Mr Morten proposed, Mr Keyworth seconded. That the letter be referred to the Charity Committee.
  Carried unanimously.

The Clerk empowered to collect the Charities — Mr Heywood proposed, Mr Lomas seconded. That the Clerk be empowered to collect the amounts due from the following six Charities, viz Vernons, Needhams, J Barbers, Bowdens, Bradshaws, and Dains.
  Carried unanimously

   Jos Heathcott
    Chairman

Meeting of The Parish Council in The Council Room.
on Monday Jany 27th 1896

Present: Mr Joseph Heathcote (presiding)

Attendance Messrs Lomas (B) Lomas (J) Keyworth, & The Clerk.

Minutes The minutes of the last meeting were read & confirmed Then signed by The Chairman.

The following letter from The County Council, was read to the Meeting

>   County Offices
>   St Marys Gate
>   Derby. 3rd January 1896
>
> The Clerk of the Parish Council
>   Chapelenlefrith
>
> Dear Sir

Letter from County Council Re Parish into Wards
I beg to inform you that the County Council are not prepared at the present time to grant the application made by your Parish Council, for the division of your parish into Wards, for Parish Council purposes.
>   Yours Faithfully
>   N J Hughes Hallet

There was also a letter read from the Charity Commissioners relating to the appointment of Trustees for Bowden Head School.

Adoption of Charity Comee Report
The report of the Charity Committee was presented Mr Heathcote proposed Mr Lomas (J) Seconded That the Report of the Charity Committee be adopted
    Carried unanimously.

Rescinding of Resolution relating to Charity Trustees appointment	Mr Keyworth proposed Mr Lomas (S) Seconded That the Resolution of the Parish Council, dated June 24th 1895 appointing Trustees for the eleven Charities viz – Walkers, Bowdens, Bradshaws, Daws, Vernon, Morsley, Gee, Gaskell, J Barber, Radcliffe, and Needham. be rescinded

Carried unanimously.

New Resolution appointing Trustees for Kirks, and Walkers Charities	Mr Lomas (B) proposed Mr Keyworth seconded. That Mr Joseph Heathcote of Chapelenlefrith, Mr Frederick Thomas Jewson Reynolds, of chapelenlefrith, Mr George Lomas of Tunstead and Mr Keyworth of Dove Holes. be appointed Trustees for Kirks, and Walkers, Charities, in place of Churchwardens and Overseers.

Carried unanimously.

New Resolution appointing Trustees for Gee's Charity	Mr Keyworth proposed Mr Lomas (B) seconded That Mr Frederick Thomas Jewson Reynolds of Chapel enlefrith and Mr George Lomas of Tunstead be appointed Trustees for Gee's Charity in place of Churchwardens

Carried unanimously

Mr Lomas (S) proposed   Mr Lomas (B) seconded
That the information required by the Charity Commissioners relating to Radcliffe's Charity be forwarded

Carried unanimously

Jos Heathcott
Chairman

Meeting of the Parish Council in the Council Room, on Monday March 6th 1896

Present   Mr Joseph Heathcott (presiding)

Attendance Messrs Lomas (B) Lomas (J), Bramwell, Spencer Keyworth, & the Clerk.

Minutes The Minutes of the last meeting were read and Confirmed.

Then signed by the Chairman.

Letter from Commissioners A Letter from the Charity Commissioners was read to the Meeting. When

Mr Keyworth proposed, Mr Bramwell seconded

Trustees for Hibbert's Charity That Mr Joseph Heathcote, Mr F. J. J. Reynolds and Mr Lomas (Tunstead) be appointed Trustees for Hibbert's Charity in place of the Overseers.

Carried unanimously.

Mr Bramwell proposed, Mr Spencer seconded
That Mr Joseph Heathcote, Mr F. J. J. Reynolds.

Trustees for Six Charities Mr G Lomas (Tunstead) and Mr G. W. Keyworth be appointed Trustees of the following Charities — Vernon's, Bowden, Bradshaws, J Barber, Dams & Needhams.

Carried unanimously.

Mr Lomas (J) proposed, Mr Spencer sec
That the following Accounts be paid.

Accounts Derbyshire County Council Expenses of Inquiry   £3 - 4 - 0
Mr Thomas Smith for Lamp &c   15. 8
The Chronicle Office for Advertisement   4 - 8
                                         ─────────
                                          4 · 4 · 4

Carried unanimously.

Arthur Heywood
      Chairman.

Meeting of the Parish Council in the Council Room on Monday March 23rd 1896

Attendance — Present Messrs Heywood, Spencer, Lomas (J) Lomas (B) Keyworth, Wain, & The Clerk

In the absence of Mr Heathcott and Mr Keyworth It was proposed by Mr Lomas (J) and seconded by Mr Spencer.

That Mr Heywood take the Chair

Carried unanimously.

Minutes — The Minutes of the last meeting were read when Mr Lomas (J) proposed Mr Lomas (B) seconded. That the minutes be confirmed.

Carried unanimously.

Remuneration for Collecting Special Rates — Mr Lomas (J) proposed Mr Spencer seconded That the Recommendation of the Overseers to allow the Assistant Overseer the sum of Ten Pounds for collecting the Special Sanitary Rate be approved

Carried unanimously.

Accounts — On the motion of Mr Spencer seconded by Mr Keyworth the following Accounts were passed.

The Savings Bank Trustees for Rent & Rates £ 2 - 7 - 11
Mr Bramwell for Printing & Books   £ 1 - 10 - 5
The Clerk &c for Stationery & Stamps   £   3 - 7

Public Tip for Dove Holes — On the Recommendation of Mr Keyworth the Council decided. That the Clerk should write to the District Council, informing them of a Suitable Place for a Public Tip for the Dove Holes district. The suggested site being in the occupation of Mr John Francis Vernon, and belonging to the Buxton Lime Firms Co

Mr Heywood then alluded to the good feeling which had existed during the Year, and Thanked the members of the Council for the kindness and consideration always shown to him.

Mr Heathcott having entered the Room. Mr Lomas (J) proposed Mr Spencer (Sec)

Vote of Thanks to Chairman

That the best thanks of the members be accorded to him for his services as Chairman during the past year.

Carried unanimously.

Mr Heathcott briefly replied and stated that he was always willing to do what he could in the Interests of the Parish and if his Services had been in any way helpful to the Council it was a pleasure to him to know it.

The meeting then Terminated

Jn Heathcott
Chairman

Annual Meeting	Annual Meeting of the Parish Council held in the Council Room on Monday April 20th 1896
Attendance	Present Mr Joseph Heathcott Messrs. Lomas (Tunstead) Lomas (Bradshaw) Keyworth Spencer, Marchington, Morten, Wain, Wild, Smith, Yates, & the Clerk.
Declarations Signed	The Declaration of Acceptance of Office was signed by each member of the Council. after which
	Mr Morten proposed Mr Wain Seconded
Provisional Chairman	That Mr George Lomas of (Tunstead) be appointed provisional Chairman
	Carried unanimously.
	Mr Morten proposed Mr Barnes Seconded
Appointment of Chairman	That Mr Joseph Heathcott be elected Chairman of the Council for the ensuing year
	Carried unanimously.
	Mr Heathcott returned thanks for the honour conferred upon him. The appointment of Overseers being the next business
Appointment of Overseers	Mr Lomas (Bradshaw) proposed Mr Lomas (Tunstead) Seconded That the Retiring Overseers viz Mr George Ibbotson
	" Mr William Ward &
	" Mr Joseph Lomas
	be re-elected as Overseers of the Poor for the Parish of Chapel-en-le-frith for the ensuing year.
	Carried unanimously.
	Mr Barnes pro Mr Morten Seconded
Appointment of Vice Chairman	That Mr George Lomas be elected Vice Chairman of the Council for the ensuing year
	Carried unanimously.
	Mr Lomas suitably Returned thanks.

Minutes — The Minutes of the last meeting were read and confirmed then signed by the Chairman.

Mr Lomas (Tunstead) proposed Mr Wain Seconded

Charities Committee — That a Charities Committee be appointed, consisting of the Chairman, Vice Chairman, Mr Mortin & Mr Keyworth.

Carried unanimously.

Mr Lomas proposed Mr Spencer Seconded

That the Charities Committee be authorized, in conjunction with the Vicar & Churchwardens, to examine any remaining documents relating to Charities, in the hands of the Vicar and Churchwardens.

Carried unanimously.

Circular Relating to Parish Highways — A Circular from the Parish Council Gazette Office, relating to the Parish Highways being under the control of the Parish Council, was read to the meeting. When

Mr Lomas (T) proposed Mr Mortin Seconded

That this Council approves of the Bill now being presented to Parliament and is of opinion that the Parish Councils are the proper authorities to take charge of their respective Parish Highways.

For — Messrs Lomas (T) Lomas (B) Mortin, Spencer, Keyworth, Wain, Marchington, Smith, Barnes.

Against — None.

Neutral — Mr Yates.

Overseers Accounts — Mr Mortin proposed Mr Keyworth seconded.

That the Accounts of the Overseers, including Mr John Cross's Account for Valuing amounting to £104-3-9 and Mr J T Gee's account amounting to £13. be approved.

Carried unanimously.

Accounts	Mr Spencer proposed Mr Keyworth Seconded
That the accounts of Mr Boycott for Election Expenses amounting to £18-11-3, and The Town Hall Trustees for Rent amounting to £1-10-0 be paid
Carried unanimously.
Precept on the Overseers	Mr Marchington proposed Mr Morten Sec
That a precept be issued on the Overseers for the Sum of £25.
Carried unanimously.
Fixing Council Meetings	Mr Morten proposed Mr Wain Seconded
That the Council Meetings be held on the 1st Monday in each of the following months — July, October, January, and April.
Carried unanimously.
Jos Heathcote
Chairman

Meeting of the Parish Council held on Monday
July 6th 1896

Present: Mr Joseph Heathcott (presiding)

Attendance — Messrs Keyworth, Barnes, Lomas (J), Smith, Yates, Spencer, Manchington & the Clerk.

Minutes — The Minutes were read and confirmed.
Then signed by the Chairman

The following is a Copy of a letter which had been received from Colonel Sidebottom M.P.   Re Highways Bill

18 Albemarle Street
London July 3rd 1896

Letter from Colonel Sidebottom re Highways — Dear Sir   I am in receipt of yours — If the Bill comes on this Session it shall have my attention and careful consideration, but I dont think there is the least chance of its being passed this year, and I would rather not absolutely pledge myself to support it.
Yours Very Truly
Wm Sidebottom

Application for consent to divert a portion of the Highway situate at White Hall — The application of Henry Shaw Esq of White Hall, for the consent of the Parish Council to a proposed diversion of a portion of the Highway leading from Whaley Bridge to Buxton, was next considered

Mr Shaw was represented by Mr Goodman, Solicitor, who produced a Map of the Highway above named and also fully explained the matter.

On the motion of Mr Lomas (J) sec by Mr Barnes the following Resolution was unanimously passed

Resolution re the diversion of a portion of Highway at White Hall.

"That on the application of Henry Shaw of White Hall in the parishes of Fernilee and Chapelenlefrith in the County of Derby Esquire the Council hereby consents that a portion of the old Highway leading from Whaley Bridge to Buxton and situate in the Parish of Fernilee within the district of the Rural District Council of Chapelenlefrith, should be stopped up and diverted viz – That so much of the said Highway as it now exists which commences at a point north of White Hall aforesaid where it is joined by the private carriage drive (passing on the north side of the Garden to the turnpike road) and passes thence in a Southeasterly direction towards Buxton as lies between the said junction with the private carriage drive and a point 415 yards southwest thereof, should shall be entirely stopped up and that the said Highway shall be diverted or turned between the said two points so as to pass to the east of the stables and outbuildings of the said Henry Shaw at White Hall aforesaid and so that the portion of the said highway so proposed to be diverted shall be of the length of 405 yards, and shall be situate in the Parish of Chapelenlefrith, instead of being of the length of 415 yards and situate in the Parish of Fernilee as at present: but if in case at any future time, Highways shall be again repaired by their respective parishes, instead of out of the general district rate as at present. Then the portion of the above mentioned highway proposed to be diverted into the Parish of Chapelenlefrith shall not be repairable by such parish.

Accounts — On the motion of Mr Keyworth sec by Mr Spencer The accounts of Mr Hunter for Chairs and the Clerk for audit Stamp amounting to £3 - 12 - 6 were passed.

Notice of Motion — Mr Smith gave notice that at the next meeting of the Council the appointment of Treasurer shall be considered.

Jos Mallicott
Chairman

Meeting of the Parish Council held on Monday October 5th 1896.

Present :— Mr Heathcott (presiding)

Attendance. Messrs Lomas (J) Lomas (B) Morten. Spencer. Barnes. Smith. Keyworth

Minutes. Proposed by Mr Keyworth. Seconded by Mr Barnes. That the minutes of the Last meeting be confirmed
Carried unanimously.

Water pollution at Sparrowpit. It was proposed by Mr Morten and Seconded by Mr Keyworth That the attention of the District Council be drawn to the Continued pollution of the water at Sparrowpit.
Carried unanimously.

Appointment of Treasurer. Proposed by Mr Lomas (J) Seconded by Mr Spencer That Mr John Taylor be appointed Treasurer of the Parish Council and that he be provided with the necessary Books. and also that the premium be paid by the Council
Carried unanimously.

Letter to be sent to Owners of Gas Works. Proposed by Mr Morten Seconded by Mr Smith That the attention of the Owners of the Gas Company and also the Lighting Inspectors be drawn to the very bad quality of the Gas as supplied to the Town. and that they be requested to take such steps as will lead to an improvement as early as possible
Carried unanimously.

The question of Better postal facilities

It was proposed by Mr Lomas (J) and Seconded by Mr Lomas (B) That in the interest of the town it is desirable to have three despatches and three deliveries of Letters during the day The first despatch to be early enough to ensure a reply the same day, and that the Clerk be instructed to communicate with Mr Bramwell, the postmaster, and request him to forward the application to the proper quarter

        Carried unanimously.

Remuneration for Collecting Special Rate

It was proposed by Mr Lomas (J) and seconded by Mr Lomas (B) That the Assistant Overseer be allowed the Sum of £10 (as recommended by the Overseers,) for Collecting the Special Sanitary Rate.

        Carried unanimously.

Accounts

Proposed by Mr Morten Seconded by Mr Lomas (J) That the following accounts be paid —
Savings Bank Trustees for Rent & Rates £2 - 5 - 5
Peter Bramwell   Caretaker   1 - 0 - 0

        Carried unanimously.

Parish Meeting to be called

Proposed by Mr Lomas (J) Seconded by Mr Keyworth That a Parish meeting be called at a convenient date to consider the division of the parish into Wards

        Carried unanimously.

        Jos Hallcott
          Chairman

Meeting of the Parish Council held in Council Office on Monday Jany 4th 1897

Present: Mr Joseph Heathcott (presiding).

Attendance — Messrs Barnes, Lomas (J), Lomas (B), Mouten, Smith.

Minutes — Proposed by Mr Lomas (J) Seconded by Mr Barnes That the minutes of the last meeting be confirmed. Carried Unanimously.

Correspondence — Letters from Mr Boycott, Re Pollution at Sparrowpit; and from Mr S J Bramwell, postmaster, referring to the Council's letter applying for better postal facilities were read to the Council. also the following letter had been received from the Charity Commissioners.

Charity Commission
1st December 1896.

County. Derby
Place. Chapelenlefrith
65945 Gaskell for Poor, Scholes and Radclyffe.
Local Government Act 1894.

Sir

Adverting to your letter of the 2nd ulto I am directed to state that in the view of the Commissioners, the Vicar, Churchwardens, and the Owner for the time being of the Martinside Estate, are the Trustees of these Charities, and that the Overseers cannot be regarded as Trustees.

Letter from Charity Commissioners Radcliffe Charity — It will therefore be competent for the Parish Council to appoint a number of Trustees in place of the Churchwardens only not exceeding the number of Churchwardens Trustees displaced.

A Copy of any Resolution of the Parish Council in the matter should be forwarded to this Office.

The deeds of 21st February and 21st April 1845, will be returned to you in the course of a few days.

I am Sir
Your Obedient Servant
G. Holford.

Mr J.J. Ford
   Clerk to Parish Council
      Chapelenlefrith

Notice of Motion — Mr Lomas (J) gave notice of Motion To appoint Two Trustees in place of Churchwardens, for Gaskell, Scholes, & Radcliffes Charity at the next Meeting.

Mr Morten proposed. Mr Smith Sec —

Valuation Charges — That the account of Mr John Cross for Valuation work, of the amount of Two Guineas be passed
      Carried unanimously.

George Lomas

Meeting of the Parish Council. held in the Council Room on Monday April 5th 1897.

Present: Mr George Lomas (Vice Chairman) presiding

Attendance — Messrs Keyworth, Smith, & Lomas (B)

On the motion of Mr Smith, Seconded by Mr Lomas (B)

Minutes — The Minutes of the last Meeting were confirmed.

A letter from the County Council relating to the Security of Treasurer to Parish Council, was read to the Council.

The following is an extract from such letter.

Extract from County Council Letter

"Ordered, that subject to the approval of the Boundaries Committee, a Treasurer of a Parish Council shall not be required to take out a Policy in a guarantee Society or give other Security where such Treasurer is an Officer in a Bank, but all such cases must be approved by the Committee."

Mr Keyworth proposed, Mr Lomas (B) Seconded. That the Clerk inform the County Council of the appointment of Mr John Taylor as Treasurer of the Chapelenlefrith Parish Council and to respectfully ask that the Order as Amended may apply in the case of such appointment.

Carried.

On the motion of the Chairman, Seconded by Mr Lomas (B)

Appointment of Two Trustees in place of Churchwardens — it was resolved that Mr Joseph Heathcote of Chapelenfrith and Mr George Lomas of Tunstead, be appointed Trustees of Gaskell's, Scholes, and Radcliffe's Charities in place of Churchwardens.

On the motion of Mr Keyworth, seconded by Mr Smith
the following Accounts were passed.

Accounts.
    Savings Bank Trustees for Rent & Gas   2 - 1 - 9
    Mr S J Bramwell (Bill   10 - 5
    Mr Jo. Brunt for Bill posting   4 - 0
    The Clerk for Stamps used   4 - 4
                                      £ 3 - 0 - 6

Vote of Thanks.
Mr Lomas (J) pro Mr Lomas (B) Sec
That a hearty Vote of Thanks be accorded to
Mr Heathcott, Chairman of the Parish Council for the
Services rendered during the past year.
        Carried.

            Jos Heathcott

Annual Meeting	Annual Meeting of the Parish Council held in the Town Hall April 21st 1897
	Present.
Attendance	Messrs Joseph Heathcott, George Lomas (T) George Lomas (B) Thomas Howarth, James C Hyde, S J Bramwell, George Ford, Edward Morten, James A Smith, George Wm Keyworth, and James Lomas.
	The declarations were signed after which
	Mr George Ford proposed Mr Morten seconded
Provisional Chairman	That George Lomas (T) be appointed provisional Chairman
	Carried
	Mr Morten proposed Mr Lomas (B) Seconded
Election Chairman	That Mr Joseph Heathcott be elected Chairman of the Parish Council for the ensuing year.
	Carried unanimously.
	Mr Heathcott then took the Chair, and returned thanks for his appointment.
	Mr Lomas (B) proposed Mr Morten sec
Vice Chairman	That Mr George Lomas of Tunstead be appointed Vice Chairman of the Council for the ensuing year
	Carried unanimously.
	Mr Lomas returned thanks for his appointment.
	The next Business was the appointment of Overseers.
Appointment of Overseers of the Poor	Mr James C Hyde pro Mr E Morten sec. That Messrs George Ibbotson, Joseph Lomas, & Tom Cooper, be appointed Overseers of the Poor for the ensuing year
	Carried unanimously.

Mr Howarth pro Mr Jas C Hyde Seconded
That a Charities Committee be appointed, consisting
of the following persons

Charities Committee
Messrs Joseph Heathcott, George Lomas (J), E Morten,
G. W. Keyworth, & S J Bramwell.
Carried unanimously.

Mr Lomas (J) pro Mr Smith Sec

Minutes
That the Minutes of the last meeting be confirmed
Carried

A Circular letter relating to the Parish Councils Highway
Bill was then read to the meeting.
After discussing the matter for some time it was
decided to defer the question until the next
meeting.

Mr Bramwell pro Mr Morten Sec.

Fixing date of Meetings
That the ordinary meetings of the Council be held
on the 1st Mondays in April, July, October, & January.
Carried unanimously.

Mr Howarth pro Mr Lomas (J) Sec

Copies of Journal to be ordered
That this Council do order Copies of the Parish Council
Journal for the year ending 15th April 1898, at an inclusive
cost of One Guinea, for the use of Members, and Officers
of the Council
Carried unanimously.

Mr Morten pro Mr Smith Sec

Returning Officers Bill
That Mr Boycotts Bill for ten Shillings be paid
Carried unanimously.

Precept for £15

Mr J C Hyde pro   Mr George Ford Seconded
That a precept be issued on the Overseers for the Sum of Fifteen pounds.
        Carried unanimously.

Charities Com'ts Meeting

Mr Howarth pro   Mr Keyworth Sec
That the Charities Committee meet in the Vestry of the Parish Church on Monday May 3rd 1897 at 7 p.m.
        Carried unanimously.

The question of a Safe for Parish documents

The question of providing a Safe for the Council was next considered but was eventually deferred until the next Meeting.

George Lomas

Meeting of the Parish Council held in the Council Office on Monday July 5th 1897.

Present: Mr George Lomas (J) presiding.

Attendance — Messrs G Lomas (B), E Morten, S J Bramwell, James C Hyde, G W Keyworth, James A Smith, George Ford, & the Clerk.

Minutes — Mr Morten proposed Mr Keyworth Seconded
That the Minutes of the last meeting be confirmed.
Carried.

Committee to inspect foot bridges — Mr Keyworth proposed Mr Bramwell Seconded.
That Messrs George Ford, Edward Morten and James A Smith, be appointed a Committee to inspect the foot bridges at Bowden Hey, Hall Heys, and Combs, and afterwards report to a later Meeting of the Council
Carried.

The following letter was read
    Charity Commission
    23rd April 1897
 County Derby.
  Place Chapel-en-le-frith
65945 Charities of Gaskell for Poor
  Scholes and Radcliffe

Letter from Charity Commission —
Local Government Act 1894.

Sir, Adverting to your letter of the 8th inst: I am directed to state that the appointments made by the parish Council of Trustees of the above named Charities in place of the Churchwardens have been duly noted in this office.
    I am Sir
Mr J J Ford   Your Obedient Servant,
 Chapel-en-le-frith   G Horford

Also the following letter from the County Offices

St Mary Gate
Derby
28th April 1897

Dear Sir

In reply to your letter of the 10th instant. I beg to inform You that at a meeting of the Boundaries Committee of the County Council held Yesterday, it was resolved, That the application made on behalf of Your Parish Council that it should not be necessary for Your Treasurer Mr John Taylor of Chapel en le frith to give Security was granted, and it was ordered that in this case the necessity for such Security was waived. You will probably require this letter for production to Your Auditor

I am Sir
Yours Faithfully
H J Hughes Hallett

Mr Joseph J Ford
Clerk to the Parish Council
Chapel en le frith

Mr George Ford proposed Mr J A Smith Sec

Application for better postal facilities

That the attention of the Postal Authorities be drawn to the fact of not having replied to the Parish Councils letter of October 1896 "re better postal facilities" and to respectfully request that the favour asked for may be granted.

Carried

Mr Lomas (B) pro Mr Morten Sec.

Letter Box for Cockyard

That the Clerk be instructed to make application to the Postal Authorities for a letter box to be placed at Cockyard.

Carried

Mr Hyde pro   Mr Geo Ford Sec.

Application for a Water Cart

That the Clerk be instructed to draw the attention of the District Council to the necessity of a Water Cart for the Town

              Carried

Mr Bramwell pro   Mr Hyde Sec.

That owing to complaints having been made about the firing of Chimneys in the daytime. The Parish Council respectfully requests the public to abstain from that practice between the hours of 6 A.M. and 10 P.M.

              Carried

Mr Bramwell pro   Mr Morten Sec

Highways Bill

That we support the Parish Councils' Highways Bill now before Parliament.

For   Messrs Bramwell, Morten, Keyworth, Lomas (B), Smith, & Ford.
Against   None
Neutral   Mr Hyde

Mr Hyde proposed   Mr George Ford Sec

A Safe to be purchased

That Mr Heathcott & Mr Bramwell be empowered to purchase a Suitable Safe for the use of the Parish Council.

              Carried.

Mr Lomas (B) pro   Mr Geo Ford Sec

The need of a Urinal

That the District Council be requested to provide a Urinal in some Suitable place on or near to the Market Ground.

              Carried

Joe Heathcott

4/10/97

Special Meeting of the Parish Council held on Monday September 20th 1897.

Present - Mr Joseph Heathcott (presiding).

Attendance — Messrs George Ford, Edward Morten, James A. Smith, James Lomas, George Lomas (J), George Lomas (B), & J J Ford.

Mr Morten proposed Mr Smith Sec

Dangerous State of Foot Bridge at Forge Bleachworks — That the Clerk be instructed to draw the attention of Mr Fleming's Solicitor to the dangerous condition of the foot bridge across the Waterway near Forge Bleachworks. and request that steps may be taken to put it in Repair.

Carried

Mr Lomas (J) proposed Mr Lomas (B) Sec

Foot Bridge at Manley Farm Combs — That the attention of the District Council be drawn to the bad state of the foot bridge near Manley Farm, leading from Combs to Buxton which we find upon enquiry has been repaired previously by the Parish Surveyors.

Carried

Mr Lomas (J) proposed Mr Lomas (B) Sec

Foot Bridge at Dam Hey Combs — That the Great Central Railway Company's attention be called to the bad condition of the Dam Hey foot bridge, near the Reservoir Combs, and request that they will be good enough to repair it.

Carried

Mr Lomas (J) proposed Mr Lomas (B) Sec

Condition of Canal Bridge Bugsworth — That the attention of the Great Central Ry Co be drawn to the dangerous state of the road on either side of the Canal Bridge at Bugsworth, owing to the unprotected state of the Canal on one side, and the Stone drops on the other

Carried

Mr George Ford pro Mr James Lomas Sec

Foot Bridge at Tunstead Milton
That the attention of John Stitt be called to the dangerous condition of a foot Bridge at Tunstead Milton through the want of protection in the form of Hand rails. and as the Bridge has recently been erected by him. he be respectfully requested to do what is necessary.
Carried.

Mr Morten proposed Mr Smith Sec

Collecting Special Rate
That the Assistant Overseer be allowed the Sum of Ten pounds (as recommended by the Overseers) for Collecting the Special Sanitary Rate
Carried unanimously.

Mr George Ford proposed Mr Lomas (I) Seconded

Remuneration to Assistant in preparing New Valuation
That the account of the Overseers payable to S. I. Bramwell of the Sum of Twenty Pounds for assistance rendered in making out and preparing New Valuation, be approved.
Carried unanimously.

Mr Morten pro Mr James Lomas Sec

Audit Stamp
That the Clerk be paid the Sum of Ten Shillings for audit Stamp.
Carried unanimously.

Jas Heathcott
4/10/97

Meeting of the Parish Council held on Monday
October 4th 1897.

Present. Mr Joseph Heathcott (presiding)

Attendance — Messrs G Lomas (T) G Lomas (B) George Ford, J A Smith, G. W. Keyworth, Thomas Howarth, Jas C Hyde, & J J Ford

Minutes

Mr Lomas (Tunstead) proposed   Mr Smith. Sec
That the Minutes of the July Meeting, and the
September Special Meeting be confirmed
              Carried unanimously.

The following letter was read to the meeting
      Chapel en le frith Rural District Council
           18th September 1897.

Dear Sir

Letter from District Council re Urinal & Water Cart

Referring to Your letter of 10th July last respecting the provision of a Urinal and the need of a Water Cart. for the town of Chapel en le frith, Your letter came before the District Council here in due course, and the matters were referred to a Committee who have them now under consideration
        Yours Truly
        J B Boycott
      Clerk to the R. D. Council.

           J R Heathcott
             Chairman
              3/1/98

Meeting of the Parish Council held on Monday
January 3rd 1898.

Attendance — Present Messrs Joseph Hathcott (presiding).
George Ford, Jas C Hyde, S J Bramwell, E Morten,
George Lomas (T), James A Smith, James Lomas, & J Ford.

Minutes — Mr Lomas (T) proposed Mr George Ford Sec
That the Minutes of the last Meeting be confirmed.
Carried.

Complaint re
foot bridge at
Tunstead Milton — Proposed by Geo Lomas Seconded by George Ford.
That the clerk be instructed to draw the attention of
Mr John Stott, to the still unsatisfactory condition of
the foot bridge at Tunstead Milton.
Carried

Notice of Motion
to appoint
Charities Trustees — Mr Hyde gave Notice of Motion to appoint Trustees, at the
next meeting, for the following Charities:-
Walker's, Bowden's, Bradshaw's, Dain's, Vernon's, J Barber's, &
Needham.

Precept — Proposed by S J Bramwell, Seconded by Jas Lomas.
That a precept be issued on the Overseers of the
poor for the Sum of £5
Carried

Cheque Book
to be ordered — Proposed by George Ford Sec by Geo Lomas.
That a Cheque Book be ordered from the
Bank.
Carried

Accounts — Proposed by S J Bramwell Sec by George Ford
That the accounts of the Savings Bank Trustees,
for Rent & Rates amounting to £2-10-2, and of
the Milners Safe Company for £21-9-0, and of
the Clerk for 2/10 for assistance rendered in fixing Safe, be paid.
Carried

Letter to be sent to Mrs A Walton Church Brow.

Proposed by E Morten Seconded by E J Bramwell That Mrs Walton's attention be drawn to the nonfulfillment of her promise, made to the parish Council on September 9th 1895, to the effect that she would as soon as possible take down the Brick Building in Church Brow, and that she be now requested to remove the Building at once.
       Carried

       E Heathcott
        4/0/98

Meeting of the Parish Council held
March 21st 1898

Attendance
Present Mr George Lomas Vice Chairman (presiding)
Messrs S J Bramwell, George Ford, E Morten
J A Smith, G W Keyworth & J S Ford

Minutes
Mr Morten proposed Mr George Ford Sec
That the Minutes of the last Meeting be confirmed
Carried

Remuneration for making out and collecting Lighting Rate
Mr Bramwell proposed Mr George Ford Seconded
That the recommendation of the Overseers "To allow the Assistant Overseer 5 per cent on amount collected, for making out and collecting Lighting Rate Aug 19/97" be approved

Accounts
Mr Morten proposed Mr Keyworth Seconded
That the following accounts be paid :-
Peter Bramwell Caretaker £1
S J Bramwell 15/4
Clerk of the peace for Register 7/9
The Clerk for Stamps 7/3
Joseph Brunt for Billposting 5/6

Meeting of the Parish Council held April 4 1898
Present Mr Joseph Heathcott (presiding)

Attendance — Messrs George Lomas (J), J Bramwell, Jas C Hyde, George Ford, E Morten, G W Keyworth, James Lomas, J A Smith, & J J Ford.

Minutes — The Minutes of the January Meeting were read and on the motion of Mr Lomas (J), seconded by E Morten they were amended to include Dixons, Kirks, Hibberts, & Sees Chamber.
The Minutes were then confirmed.

Foot bridge at Hall Heys — Mr Lomas proposed Mr Smith seconded That the attention of Mr Fleming's Solicitors be drawn to the fact of the Bridge at Hall Heys not yet having been repaired, and that they be requested to carry out the work as soon as possible
Carried

Letter to be sent to Mrs Walton Church Brow — Mr Bramwell proposed Mr Hyde Sec That Mrs Walton of Church Brow be reminded that she has not yet carried out her promise viz. to take down the Brick Building and restore the site to the road, and that she be requested to attend to the matter as early as possible.
Carried.

Foot Bridge at Burrfields — Mr Morten proposed Mr Smith Sec That the attention of Mr John Bennett of Stodhart be drawn to the dangerous state of the foot bridge opposite New houses, owing to the want of protection, and that he be respectfully requested to do what is necessary
Carried.

Proposed by Mr Keyworth   Seconded by Mr Lomas (T)

Appointment of Trustee for Gee's Charity — That Mr George Ford be appointed Trustee for Gee's Charity, in place of Mr Reynolds, whose name was drawn out by lot.

Carried

Mr S J Bramwell pro   Mr Jas Lomas sec

Trustees for Walkers Charity — That Messrs Jas C Hyde, & Edward Morten be appointed Trustees for Walkers Charity, in lieu of Mr Lomas (T) & Mr Keyworth, whose names were drawn out by lot.

Carried

pro Mr Bramwell   Sec Mr Hyde

Trustees for Vernons & Bowdens Charities — That Messrs J A Smith & James Lomas, be appointed Trustees for Vernons & Bowdens Charities in lieu of Lomas (T) & Keyworth, drawn out.

Carried

pro Mr Morten   Sec Mr Smith

Trustees for J Barbers Charity — That Messrs S J Bramwell & Francis Bramwell be appointed Trustees for J Barbers Charity in place of Lomas & Keyworth, drawn out.

Carried

pro Mr Bramwell   Sec Mr Morten

Trustees for Bradshaw Charity — That George Lomas (T) & George Lomas (B) be appointed Trustees for Bradshaws Charity, in lieu of Lomas & Keyworth drawn out.

Carried

Mr Smith pro   Mr Bramwell Sec

Trustees for Davis & Needham Charities — That Messrs Geo Lomas (T) & G W Keyworth be re-appointed Trustees for Davis & Needham Charities.

Carried

Mr Bramwell pro   Mr Morten Sec

Trustees for Kirks Charity That Messrs Joseph Heathcott & G W Keyworth be reappointed Trustees for Kirks Charity

Carried

Mr Morten pro   Mr Keyworth Sec

Trustees for Hibberts Charity That Messrs Jas C Hyde & S J Bramwell be appointed Trustees for Hibberts Charity in lieu of Mr Heathcott & Mr Lomas. (J)

Carried

Mr Bramwell pro   Mr Hyde Sec

Trustee for Educational Charities That Mr James Thomason be reappointed Trustee for Dixons Marchingtons & Kirks, Educational Charity.

Carried

Votes of thanks On the motion of Mr Lomas (J) Sec by Mr Morten a hearty vote of thanks was accorded to Mr Heathcott for his Services as Chairman during the past year.

Vote of thanks On the motion of Mr Bramwell Sec by Mr Smith a hearty vote of thanks was accorded to Mr Lomas (J) for his Services as Vice Chairman during the past year.

Jos Heathcott
18/4/95

1898

Annual Meeting — Annual Meeting of the Parish Council held on Monday April 18th 1898.

Attendance — Present. Messrs. George Ford, S J Bramwell, G W Keyworth, J A Smith, I C Hyde, George Lomas (J), E Morten, Francis Bramwell, & J J Ford.

The declarations were signed, after which

Provisional Chairman — Mr Hyde proposed Mr Lomas Sec That S J Bramwell be appointed provisional Chairman.
Carried.

Chairman Elect — Mr Lomas proposed Mr Keyworth Seconded That Mr Joseph Heathcott be appointed Chairman of the Parish Council for the ensuing year.
Carried unanimously.

Mr Heathcott briefly returned thanks.

Proposed by George Ford, Seconded by S J Bramwell.

Vice Chairman — That George Lomas (J) be appointed Vice Chairman for the ensuing year.
Carried unanimously.

Mr Lomas returned thanks for his appointment.

Appointment of Overseers — Proposed by George Lomas, Seconded by E Morten, That Messrs George Ibbotson, Joseph Lomas, and Tom Cooper, be re-appointed Overseers of the poor for the ensuing year.
Carried unanimously.

Minutes of Annual Meeting Cont'd.

Proposed by George Lomas, Sec by George Ford

Minutes — That the Minutes of the last meeting be confirmed.
Carried

Proposed by George Ford, Seconded by J A Smith,

Foot Bridge at Hall Heys — That the Solicitors of Mr Fleming be again written to in reference to the foot bridge at Hall Heys. and they be requested to do what is necessary without further delay.
Carried.

Proposed by J C Hyde, Sec by J. Bramwell

Encroachment Church Brow — That inasmuch as Mrs Walton has not carried out the resolution of the Council, she be again requested to restore the site of the Brick Building in Church Brow, to its original state.
Carried unanimously.

Foot Bridge Burnfield — Proposed by George Lomas, Sec by S J Bramwell
That Mr John Bennett be again written to in reference to foot bridge at Burnfields.

Carried

Proposed by S J Bramwell Sec by J. A. Smith.

Parish Council Journal — That this Council do order Copies of the Parish Council Journal for the year ending 15 April 1899 at an inclusive cost of One guinea, for the use of Members and Officers of the Council.
Carried

Proposed by George Ford, Sec by S J Bramwell

Precept — That a precept be served on the Overseers of the poor for the Sum of Ten pounds (£10.)

Carried

Proposed by J A Smith, Sec by George Lomas
That the Two absent members be permitted to sign the declaration at the next meeting of the Council.

Carried

Proposed by E Morten, Sec by G W Keyworth.

Committee to name Streets &c. — That the following members be appointed a Committee to go into the question of naming the streets and numbering the houses.

Joseph Heathcott
L C Hyde
George Ford
S J Bramwell
Francis Bramwell

Carried unanimously

Proposed by S J Bramwell   Sec by F Bramwell.

Accounts — That the following Accounts be paid.
Savings Bank Trustees Rent & Rates £2 - 3 - 1
Parish Councils Association   £1 - 1 - 0

Carried

J Heathcott
4/7/98

Meeting of the Parish Council held on Monday July 4th 1898.

Present Mr Joseph Heathcott (presiding),

Attendance — Messrs S J Bramwell, J C Hyde, F Bramwell, George Ford, G Lomas (B), J A Smith, James Lomas, E Moston, & J J Ford.

Minutes — J C Hyde proposed F Bramwell seconded That the Minutes of the last Meeting be confirmed
Carried.

Foot Bridge at Hall Hey — Pro by J A Smith, Sec by George Ford That the question of repairing foot Bridges at Hall Hey and Burnfields be adjourned until further information is obtained, when a Special Meeting may be held.

Encroachment in Church Brow — Mrs Walton's reply to our letter in reference to the supposed encroachment in Church Brow, was read considered, but nothing was done in the Matter.

Naming of Streets — Proposed by S J Bramwell, Sec by George Ford That the report of the Street-Naming Committee be adopted, and that the District Council be requested to carry out the recommendations of the Committee in reference to the naming of Streets.
Carried

Notice Boards — Proposed by George Ford. Sec by J A Smith That the District Council be requested to fix Notice Boards or plates, opposite the post office, and at the end of Long Lane, directing passengers to the L & N.W. Ry Station.
Carried.

Proposed by J C Hyde   Sec by E Morten

Remuneration for Collecting Special Rate
That the Recommendation of the Overseers, to allow the Assistant Overseer the Sum of Ten pounds, for making out and collecting Special Expenses Rate, be confirmed. (Rate made Apl 26/98)
Carried

Proposed by J C Hyde   Sec by E Morten

Remuneration for collecting Lighting Rate
That the Recommendation of the Overseers, to allow the Assistant Overseer the Sum of Four pounds for making out and collecting Lighting Rate be confirmed. (Rate made May 21/98)
Carried

Mr Heathcott proposed   Mr Smith Sec
That J B Boycott's Account for 10/- be paid
Carried

Letter box Cockyard
Proposed by George Lomas (B) Seconded by James Lomas
That the postal Authorities be asked to provide Wall letter boxes at Cockyard, and Slack Hall.
Carried.

B Heathcott
3/10/98

Special Meeting — Special Meeting of the Parish Council held on Friday July 15th 1898.

Present

Attendance — Messrs Jos. Heathcott, J C Hyde, S J Bramwell, George Ford, J A Smith, G Lomas (J), James Lomas, J Bramwell, G W Keyworth, & J J Ford.

Proposed by S J Bramwell Seconded by —

Alleged pollution of Water Supply at Town End — That owing to complaints having been made by a number of Ratepayers in reference to an alleged pollution of the Water Supply at Town End, the District Council be recommended to investigate the Matter.

Carried.

Jos Heathcott
3/10/98

Meeting of the Parish Council held Monday October 3 1898.

Present: Mr Heathcote (presiding)
Messrs J. C. Hyde, George Ford, G W Keyworth, James A Smith, George Lomas (T) and George Lomas (B).

Proposed by George Lomas (T) sec by G W Keyworth That the Minutes of the July Meeting be confirmed.
Carried.

Proposed by George Lomas (T) sec by F Bramwell.

That the Accounts of the Clerk for 10/- Audit Stamp, and Peter Bramwell's Account of £1 for Caretaking be paid.
Carried.

Jos Heathcote

Special Meeting — Special Meeting of the Parish Council held on Monday January 2nd 1899.

Attendance — Present Mr Heathcott (presiding) Messrs George Lomas (T) George Lomas (B) I C Hyde, George Ford, F Bramwell, S J Bramwell, J A Smith.

Election of Parish Councillor — Business: To Elect a Parish Councillor in place of the late Edward Morten.

It was proposed by Mr Heathcott and Seconded by George Lomas (T)

Letter of Condolence — That the Clerk be instructed to forward a letter of Sympathy to the Widow and family of the late Edward Morten in their bereavement.

Carried.

Proposed by George Lomas (B) Seconded by George Lomas (T)

Mr Tom Cooper Elected — That Mr Tom Cooper of Blackbrook be elected a Parish Councillor in place of the late Edward Morten.

Carried there voting
For the resolution. Five
Against None
Neutral Two

Jos Heathcott
Chairman

Ordinary Meeting of the Parish Council held at 7.30 on Monday Jany 2nd 1899

Attendance.

Messrs Joseph Heathcote, George Lomas (J) George Lomas (B) J C Hyde, George Ford, T Bramwell, S Bramwell, J A Smith, and J J Ford.

On the Motion of George Ford Sec by George Lomas it was resolved

That the Minutes of the Ordinary and later Special Meetings be confirmed.

Carried

The following letter was read from the Furnilee Parish Council

Furnilee. Whaley Bridge
Dec 22 1898.

Dear Sir

In consequence of the danger to the public, during the Winter, in passing over the level crossing at Lane End, Whaley Bridge. The above Council propose to ask the L & N W Ry Company to provide and erect a lamp at this place, and I am requested to ask you, if your Council will kindly assist us as it is thought a joint request from both Councils may induce the Company to do what is requisite in the matter.

Yours Faithfully
Samuel Bennett. Clerk.

It was proposed by the Chairman and Seconded by George Ford

That the assistance asked for by the Furnilee Parish Council in the above letter be granted.

Carried.

On the Motion of the Vice Chairman, Seconded by
J C Hyde it was Resolved:

Railway Companies
to provide foot
Bridges or
underground passages

That the Clerk be instructed to draw the attention
of the Two Railway Companies, to the desirability of
providing Bridges, or underground passages at their
respective Stations, for the Safety of passengers

Carried.

George Lomas JP proposed J Bramwell Sec
That the following Accounts be paid:

Accounts

		£	s	d
Savings Bank Trustees	rent & rates	2	4	10
J Bramwell	Posters for Parish Meeting held Oct 3rd 1898		3	6
Joseph Brunt	Bill posting for Parish Meeting		4	0

Jas Heathcott
Chairman

Meeting of the Parish Council held on Monday April 3rd 1899

Attendance — Present: The Chairman, Vice Chairman, Messrs J C Hyde, George Ford, S J Bramwell, Tom Cooper, G W Keyworth, James Lomas, Francis Bramwell, James A Smith, & J J Ford

Minutes — On the motion of the Vice Chairman, seconded by George Ford the Minutes of the last Meeting were confirmed.

The following letter from Mr Boycott was read.

Chapel-en-le-Frith 8th Feb 1899

Dear Sir

Letter from Mr Boycott

"Re Burrfields Road"

Burrfields Road

I send you herewith a Memorial signed by a large number of inhabitants addressed to the District Council in reference to the above road, and praying for some steps to be taken to have a properly formed footpath made along it. The question was taken into consideration at the last meeting of the Council when a general opinion was expressed that this was one of those matters which could more properly be dealt with by your Council than the District Authority, and I was directed to ask your Council to be good enough to take the matter in hand and see what can be done to comply with the request of the Memorialists. Possibly if your Council appointed a deputation to confer with the land owners on the subject, some satisfactory arrangement could be arrived at.

I shall be happy to help you in any way that I can but I trust you will experience no insuperable difficulties in giving effect to the views of the petitioners.

Believe me
Yours faithfully
S. R. Boycott

Mr J J Ford
Clerk to Parish Council

The following is a copy of the petition referred to by Mr Boycott in his letter.

Copy of Petition referred to in Mr Boycott's letter.

We the undersigned beg to petition the Rural District Council of the Parish of Chapel-en-le-frith, to cause a good public footpath to be made along the road situate in Burrfields, extending from the Church Yard Gates, to the Hayfield Road, opposite the Grapes Inn. During wet weather in all seasons, this road is in a most disgraceful state, & not only causes great annoyance & inconvenience to the residents in Burrfields, but also to the numerous foot passengers who make constant use of it; besides being a real source of danger to the School Children who are obliged to use the road, and get their feet wet before school begins.

Signed by One hundred persons.

Comtee Appointed

On the Motion of G W Keyworth, Sec by James Lomas Messrs George Lomas, S J Bramwell, and Francis Bramwell were appointed a Committee to confer with the owners of the land upon the subject, and see what can be done in the matter.

Carried

Resolution Re Water Supply

S J Bramwell proposed F. Bramwell Seconded.
That in the opinion of the Parish Council, the District Council should lose no time in taking the necessary steps to place the water supply of Chapel-en-le-frith in a satisfactory condition

Carried.

George Lomas (?) proposed George Ford seconded That the recommendation of the Overseers of the poor to allow Joseph Goddard the sum of Thirty pounds for making a survey of the Parish and preparing a list of Field Measurements for the Rate Book and Valuation List, be confirmed.

   Carried unanimously.

Precept Proposed by the Vice Chairman Seconded by S J Bramwell That a precept be issued upon the Overseers of the poor for the sum of £25

   Carried unanimously.

The following Accounts were passed for payment :-

Accounts

	£ s d
Savings Bank Trustees (Rent & jnitos)	£2 - 2 - 2
S J Bramwell Stationery	" 19 - 0
The Clerk of the Peace	2 - 10
I I Ford for stamps used during year	7 - 4
	£3 - 11 - 4

Votes of Thanks On the motion of George Lomas seconded by I A Smith, a hearty vote of thanks was accorded to the Chairman for his services during the past year. and also to the Vice Chairman on the motion of I C Hyde seconded by Francis Bramwell.

Annual Meeting	Annual Meeting of the Parish Council held April 17, 1899
Attendance	Present Messrs J C Hyde, F. Bramwell, Tom Cooper, John Hague, George Lomas (J) James Lomas, G W Keyworth, J A Smith & J G Ford.
Temporary Chairman	The declarations having been signed Mr Lomas (J) proposed, Mr Hyde Sec — That the Clerk be appointed temporary chairman Carried unanimously.
Election of Chairman	Proposed by Mr Hyde Seconded by Mr Lomas That Mr Joseph Heathcott be appointed Chairman of the Parish Council for the ensuing year. Carried unanimously.
Election of Vice Chairman	Proposed by Mr Tom Cooper, Seconded by J A Smith That George Lomas (J) be appointed Vice Chairman of the Parish Council for the ensuing year Carried unanimously
Overseers	Proposed by George Lomas, Seconded by Francis Bramwell That Messrs Joseph Lomas, George Ibbotson, and Tom Cooper be appointed Overseers of the poor for this Parish for the ensuing year Carried unanimously.
Minutes	On the Motion of Francis Bramwell, Seconded by the Vice Chairman The Minutes of the last Meeting were confirmed.

James Lomas proposed Tom Cooper Seconded
That the following accounts be paid –

Accounts:
    J B Boycott £18"6"0 Election Expenses
    Joseph Bryant 5/6 for Bill posting
    The Clerk 5/- for Audit Stamp

              Carried unanimously.

Notice of Motion
Mr Lomas (J) gave notice of Motion to consider at the next meeting the desirability of dividing the parish into Wards on similar lines to the last attempt.

Declaration
Mr Hyde proposed Mr Smith Sec
That Messrs S J Bramwell & George Lomas (B) be allowed to sign the declarations at the next Meeting
              Carried.

Journals to be ordered
Proposed by Mr Smith Seconded by Mr Bramwell
That the Council do order Copies of the Councils Journal for the year ending 15th April 1900 at an inclusive cost of One Guinea for the use of Members and Officers of the Council
              Carried unanimously.

Account for Journals
Proposed by the Vice Chairman Seconded by Mr Smith
That the account of One Guinea for Journals be paid
              Carried unanimously.

Meeting of the Parish Council held on Monday July 3 1899.

Attendance — Present Messrs Joseph Heathcote, George Lomas (T) George Lomas (B) J C Hyde, S J Bramwell, John Hague, Frank Bramwell, G W Keyworth, J A Smith, Tom Cooper

Minutes — The Minutes were read and on the motion of John Hague seconded by George Lomas, they were confirmed.

Notice of Motion Withdrawn — Mr Lomas did not desire to proceed with his notice of Motion Re the desirability of dividing the parish into Wards, consequently it was withdrawn.

Petition Re Branch Post Office at Town End — A Petition signed by 67 inhabitants of the east end of the town, requesting the Parish Council to take steps to secure a Branch Post Office at Town End, was next considered. After discussing the matter J C Hyde proposed G Lomas (B) seconded the following resolution:—

Petition to be supported — That the petition be supported, and that the Clerk be instructed to make the proper application to the Authorities, also that a request be made at the same time for a pillar box to be erected near to Mr Woodcock's Shop, and another near to the Grapes Inn.

Carried unanimously.

Resolution Re proposed 3rd delivery of letters	Mr Hague proposed George Lomas Sec That the Clerk write to the postal Authorities requesting that in view of the contemplated third delivery we ask that it may be later than the present night delivery. Carried unanimously
Salary For Collecting Sanitary Rate	Proposed by G Lomas (J) Seconded by S J Bramwell That the recommendation of the Overseers to allow the Assistant Overseer the sum of Ten pounds for collecting the Sanitary Rate (made May 4" 1899) be approved Carried unanimously.
Salary for Collecting Lighting Rate	Proposed by John Hague Seconded by G Lomas (B) That the recommendation of the Overseers to allow the Assistant Overseer the sum of Four pounds for collecting the Lighting Rate (made June 22") be approved. Carried unanimously.
Application for increase of Salary of Ass't Overseer	The Council next considered an application for an increase of Salary from the Assistant Overseer, when Mr Heathcote proposed Mr Cooper Seconded. That the appointment of the Assistant Overseer be revoked. Carried.
Salary increased to £35	Proposed by Mr Heathcote Seconded by George Lomas (J) That Joseph James Ford be appointed Assistant Overseer for the Parish of Chapel-en-le-frith at a Salary of Thirty five pounds per annum. Carried unanimously.

www.ingramcontent.com/pod-product-compliance
Lightning Source LLC
Chambersburg PA
CBHW081918090526
44590CB00019B/3395